English
At Your Command!

Practice Book

HAMPTON-BROWN

Table of Contents

Color, Size, and Shape Words

📖 Use Handbook pages 14–15.

- Look at the objects in your classroom, at school, or at home.

- Write sentences to tell about their colors, sizes, and shapes.

1. The basketball is round. It is orange and black.

2. The box is a square. It is brown.

3. _____

4. _____

5. _____

6. _____

Number Words

 Use Handbook page 16.

- Draw a picture of something that has a number on it.
- Use number words to write the number.

1.

two thousand nine hundred
sixty-three

4.

_____

_____

2.

_____

_____

5.

_____

_____

3.

_____

_____

6.

_____

_____

Order Words/More Words That Tell How Many

📖 **Use Handbook page 17.**

■ **Read the story.**

■ **Write a word from the box to finish each sentence.**

On June ___fourth___ my family had a big birthday
           1

party to celebrate everyone's

birthday at the same time.

My grandmother had her _____ birthday in
                               2

February. We gave her a _____ of purple slippers.
                               3

Aunt Marta turned forty on the eighth of April. It was her

_____ birthday. We gave her _____
       4   **5**

of books. Uncle Robert's birthday was a _____
                                                6

days after Aunt Marta's. He got a new golf club and

_____ golf balls.
       7

At the party, we sang "Happy Birthday" _____
                                                8

times and played games. Before everyone left, we agreed to

celebrate again next year.

fortieth
pair
seventieth
some
few
several
fourth
a lot

Sensory Words

📖 **Use Handbook pages 18–19.**

- **Draw a picture of your favorite meal.**

- **Write sentences to tell how each food looks, feels, smells, sounds, and tastes.**

_____

_____

_____

_____

_____

_____

Feeling Words

📖 Use Handbook page 20.

- **Read the feeling word.**

- **Write a sentence about a time you felt that way.**

1. angry   *I was angry when my toy spaceship* _____
      fell apart. _____

2. bored _____
_____

3. sad _____
_____

4. happy _____
_____

5. puzzled _____
_____

6. surprised _____
_____

7. embarrassed _____
_____

8. afraid _____
_____

- **Now tell about two other feelings you have had.**

9. I felt _____ when _____
_____

10. I felt _____ when _____
_____

Words That Tell Where

📖 Use Handbook page 21.

- **Look at the picture.**

- **Choose a word from the box to finish each sentence. Tell about the picture.**

1. Player 3 is in _____*front of*_____ the net.

2. The ball is _____ the ground.

3. The ball is _____ Players 1 and 3.

4. Player 1 is _____ the bench.

5. A pair of shoes is _____ the bench.

6. There is a hat _____ the bag.

7. A big water bottle is _____ the bench.

8. Player 2 is _____ the bench.

far away from
behind
between
front of
inside
next to
on
under

© Hampton-Brown

Multiple-Meaning Words

📖 Use Handbook pages 23–26.

- ■ Write a word from Handbook pages 23–26 for each picture. Write the part of speech for the word.

- ■ Then write a sentence using the word.

1.   bat, noun   I hit a home run with my new baseball bat.

2.

3.

4.

5.

6.

7.

8.

Multiple-Meaning Words

📖 Use Handbook pages 26–28.

- **Read each sentence.**
- **Mark the correct meaning of the word in dark print.**

1. Last year I **left** Vietnam and came to my new school.
   - ⬤ went away from
   - ◯ opposite of right
   - ◯ remaining

2. My teacher was **Miss** Adams.
   - ◯ to long for
   - ◯ an unmarried woman
   - ◯ to not hit a target

3. She asked me to **point** to my home country on the map.
   - ◯ show
   - ◯ a dot on a line
   - ◯ a statement

4. Then she drew a **ring** around it with a red pen.
   - ◯ circle
   - ◯ jewelry for the finger
   - ◯ the sound of a bell

5. Next, I showed the class my special **ring**.
   - ◯ a circle
   - ◯ jewelry for the finger
   - ◯ the sound of a bell

6. I always wear it on my **left** hand.
   - ◯ went away from
   - ◯ opposite of right
   - ◯ remaining

7. When the bell began to **ring** we went out to play jump rope.
   - ◯ a circle
   - ◯ jewelry for the finger
   - ◯ make the sound of a bell

8. I **miss** my friends in Vietnam, but I love my new home and school.
   - ◯ long for
   - ◯ to not hit a target
   - ◯ an unmarried woman

Similes

📖 Use Handbook page 30.

- **Look at the two pictures. Read the question.**
- **Write the answer. Use a simile.**

1. What are Mr. Ruiz's hands as cold as?

Mr. Ruiz's hands are as cold as ice.

4. What is the scarf as warm as?

_____

_____

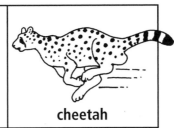

2. How does Mary Jane run?

_____

_____

5. How does Jake jump?

_____

_____

3. How does Mrs. Smith sing?

_____

_____

6. What is Tony as strong as?

_____

_____

© Hampton-Brown

Sound-Alike Words

📖 **Use Handbook pages 32–34.**

■ **Read each sentence.**

■ **Choose the correct word below the line.**
  Write the word in the blank.

1. Antonio's ____*aunt*____ always gives him a special gift for his birthday.

aunt / ant

2. This year she decided to _____ him concert tickets.

by / buy

3. She bought _____ tickets so he could invite some friends.

four / for

4. The tickets were _____ seats by the stage.

four / for

5. Antonio was going to _____ his favorite band!

see / sea

6. The show would start at _____ o'clock.

ate / eight

7. They would leave after they _____ dinner.

ate / eight

8. It would take an _____ to drive to the amphitheater.

hour / our

9. The amphitheater was _____ the airport.

by / buy

10. Antonio couldn't wait for the concert day to get _____!

hear / here

Synonyms

📖 **Use Handbook pages 35–37.**

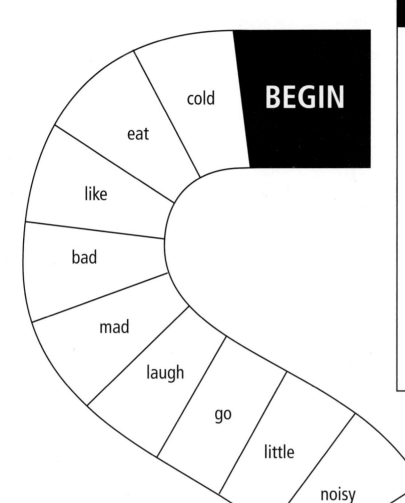

The board game spaces read: BEGIN, cold, eat, like, bad, mad, laugh, go, little, noisy, afraid, happy, good, big, brave, cry, THE END

How to Play
The Synonym Game

1. Play with a partner.

2. Use an eraser or other small object as your game piece. Use a coin to show how many spaces to move.

    Heads = 1 space

    Tails = 2 spaces

3. Say the word in the space.

4. Say a synonym for the word. Then use the synonym in a sentence. For example: *cold–freezing. It's **freezing** outside.*

5. The first one to reach **THE END** wins.

Synonyms

📖 **Use Handbook pages 35–39.**

- ■ **Read the paragraph. Look at the underlined words.**

- ■ **Rewrite the paragraph. Replace the underlined words with synonyms.**

     I <u>like</u> soccer! Last night my mom and I went to a soccer match. I was <u>happy</u> to be there. It was <u>cold</u> outside, so I got a <u>warm</u> drink. I <u>ate</u> a hamburger, too. The Seahawks were playing well. All their players are <u>strong</u>. When they <u>go</u> down the field, no one can stop them. When the Seahawks scored the first goal, the crowd started to <u>talk</u>. The cheering was <u>noisy</u>. It started to rain, but the game was so <u>good</u> that no one wanted to go home until the end!

_____

_____

_____

_____

_____

_____

_____

_____

_____

_____

_____

_____

Antonyms

📖 Use Handbook pages 40–41.

- Write a word from Handbook pages 40–41 in the box. Then write a sentence using the word.

- Ask your partner to write the antonym for the word and write a sentence using the antonym.

1. clean My shirt is clean.	dirty My shoes are dirty.
2.	
3.	
4.	
5.	
6.	

Time and Measurement

Use Handbook pages 42–43.

- Read the questions.
- Write the answers. Use time words.

1. When do you wake up?

I wake up at six o'clock daily.

2. When do you eat breakfast on school days?

_____

3. When do you leave for school?

_____

4. When do you eat lunch?

_____

5. When do you get home from school?

_____

6. When do you do your homework?

_____

7. When do you have dinner?

_____

8. When do you go to bed?

_____

9. What do you do on Saturdays?

_____

10. What is your favorite time of day?

_____

Time and Measurement

📖 Use Handbook page 45.

- Use a ruler or a scale to measure or weigh six things in the classroom.

- Complete the chart.

What I Measured or Weighed	What I Learned About It
1. my English book	It is 8 inches wide and 10 inches long. It weighs 2 pounds, 3 ounces.
2. _____	_____
3. _____	_____
4. _____	_____
5. _____	_____
6. _____	_____

Compound Words

📖 Use Handbook pages 46–47.

- Look at the picture.
- Make compound words to tell about the picture. Use the words in the boxes.

1. _summertime_

2. _____

3. _____

4. _____

5. _____

First Part	+	Second Part
summer		shine
out		noon
back		time
sun		side
after		yard

6. _____

7. _____

8. _____

9. _____

10. _____

First Part	+	Second Part
lunch		burgers
table		apple
ham		time
water		melon
pine		cloth

Suffixes

📖 Use Handbook pages 48–50.

- **Read each sentence.**

- **Mark the suffix that can be added to the word. Then write the word with the suffix.**

1. My Aunt Celia has a **convert**___ car.
  ◯ -ment   ⬤ -ible   ◯ -ful

convertible

2. She is a very good **drive**___.
  ◯ -er   ◯ -ion   ◯ -ward

_____

3. Today she took me **west**___ to Lake Paz.
  ◯ -ward   ◯ -ion   ◯ -en

_____

4. I could see the sun's **reflect**___ on the water.
  ◯ -less   ◯ -ness   ◯ -ion

_____

5. Later, the sky began to **dark**___.
  ◯ -tion   ◯ -able   ◯ -en

_____

6. I was full of **sad**___ as it began to rain!
  ◯ -ment   ◯ -ness   ◯ -ful

_____

7. We had to put up the top, but Aunt Celia was **cheer**___.
  ◯ -ful   ◯ -ment   ◯ -ward

_____

8. She said the rain was **harm**___.
  ◯ -ness   ◯ -er   ◯ -less

_____

9. We made an **agree**___ to return next week!
  ◯ -less   ◯ -ment   ◯ -er

_____

Prefixes

📖 Use Handbook pages 51–53.

- ■ Read each sentence.
- ■ Use a word with a prefix to replace the words below the blank.
- ■ Write the word with the prefix.

1. For my birthday party, I wanted to ride my _____bicycle_____

two-wheeled cycle
   with my friends.

2. My friends were excited as we _____ the party.

planned before

3. We always have fun and _____ well.

work together

4. We _____ the park, so we decided to ride at the beach.

do not like

5. Dad took us there in his _____ .

small van

6. We rode _____ until the sun set!

without stopping

7. Then, we _____ our bikes to the van and went home.

attached again

8. I will write about that special day in my _____!

biography about myself

Word Families

📖 Use Handbook pages 54–55.

- ■ **Read each sentence.**
- ■ **Choose a word from the box to finish each sentence. Write the word in the blank.**
- ■ **Circle the root word.**

> incorrect
> governor
> international
> grown-up
> national
> correction
> government
> nation

1. Kysha is a very good speller. She hardly ever gives any

_____ in(correct) _____ answers at the school spelling bee.

2. Her teacher rarely makes a _____ on

Kysha's spelling tests.

3. Kysha can spell almost as well as a _____.

4. Now she is going to a _____ spelling bee!

5. Kids from around the _____ compete to be

the Best Speller in the country.

6. If Kysha wins, she will go to an _____

spelling bee with kids from around the world.

7. Bob Liu, our state _____, called

to wish Kysha good luck!

8. Mayor Bix called, too. She's the leader of our city

_____.

Idioms

📖 Use Handbook pages 58–60.

- ■ **Work with a partner.**

- ■ **Look at each picture. Write words from the box to finish what the girls are saying.**

1.

> Give it your best shot!   I'm all thumbs!
> I've got cold feet.   Break a leg!

I can't go out there! _____
_____
_____
_____

Don't worry. _____
_____
_____

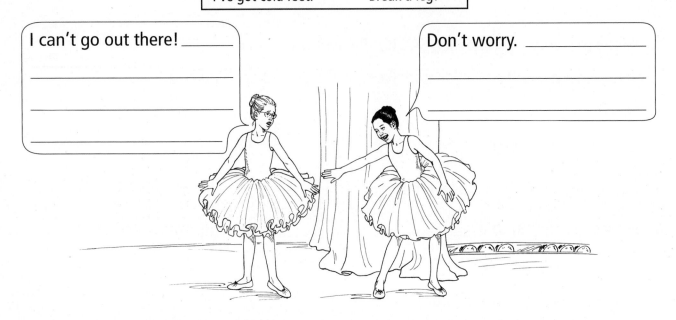

2.

> That was as easy as pie.   I was as cool as a cucumber.
> Now, pat yourself on the back!   I said it would be a piece of cake.

Wow! I did it. _____
_____
_____
_____

I knew you could do it.
_____
_____
_____

Idioms

📖 Use Handbook pages 60–61.

- ■ **Work with a partner.**
- ■ **Finish what the boys are saying. Use words from the boxes.**

1.

| lend you a hand | in a jam | upside down | keep your shirt on |

I'm _in a jam_. I can't find my baseball card to trade. I've turned the room _____!

I'll _____ .
Just _____ !

2.

| You bet | pat ourselves on the back | put our heads together | off the hook |

I found it!
I'm _____ .
When we _____
_____ , we can do anything!

_____we can.
We should _____ _____ .

Two-Word Verbs

📖 Use Handbook pages 62–63.

- Read each sentence. Look at the verb in dark print.

- Choose the correct word below the line to make a two-word verb. Write the word in the blank.

1. We heard something **breaking**

    ___*up*___ inside our car's
    <u>out / up</u>

    engine on Saturday.

2. Then the car **broke** _____ , and
    <u>down / up</u>

    Dad and I had to walk everywhere.

3. First, we **checked** _____ on
    <u>off / up</u>

    Grandma to see if she was okay.

4. At Grandma's, we phoned Mom to **check** _____ with her.
    <u>off / in</u>

5. She **brought** _____ ideas for places to go, such as the library and the store.
    <u>off / up</u>

6. At the library, I **filled** _____ a form for a library card.
    <u>off / out</u>

7. At the store, Dad **brought** _____ the grocery list.
    <u>out / on</u>

8. We **checked** _____ everything on the list, and then we carried
    <u>up / off</u>

    the groceries home.

© Hampton-Brown

Two-Word Verbs

📖 Use Handbook pages 64–65.

■ **Look at each picture. Read the sentence.**

■ **Write a two-word verb from the box in the blank.**

get over	give up	go away
get out	look over	give back

1. I hope I __*get over*__ this cold soon.

2. I always _____ my homework before I turn it in.

3. I have to _____ my library book.

4. I want the rain to _____ so I can play outside.

5. I _____ of the bus at the corner near my house.

6. I won't _____ until I make ten baskets!

Two-Word Verbs

📖 Use Handbook pages 62–67.

- Read the story.

- Write a two-word verb from the box in each blank.

Maria is ___going away___ for a week
                    1

to Space Camp. She has been _____
                                    2

to this for a long time. Marc went last year and said it was so

much fun that he wanted to _____ there.
                                3

Last winter, Maria _____ an application.
                          4

The camp sent her lots of information to _____.
                                                5

looking forward
go back
going away
look over
filled out

Yesterday, Maria packed. She _____ just
                                    6

the right clothes to wear. She carefully _____
                                              7

each item from a list that the camp sent her.

Maria has to _____ at the camp very early
                  8

Monday morning. So she _____ the light
                              9

and gets into bed. Maria can't go to sleep, though. She keeps

_____ and over because she's so excited
       10

about her trip!

check in
turns off
picked out
turning over
checked off

© Hampton-Brown

Character Map

📖 Use Handbook page 70.

- **Think about a character from a story you have read.**

- **Make a character map to show what that character is like.**

- **Now cover up the name of your character and show the character map to a partner. Can your partner guess who the character is?**

Event Cluster

📖 Use Handbook page 71.

- Think about a community event you have been to.

- Fill in the cluster. Write the name of the event. Then write details that tell more about the event.

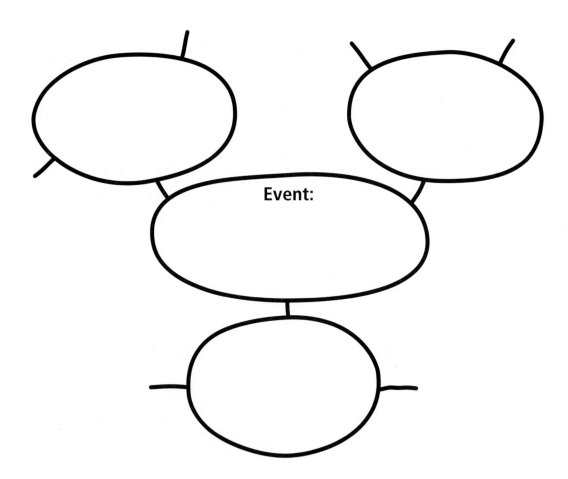

Event:

- Now, cover up the name of the event. Ask a partner to guess the event.

Parts Diagram
📖 Use Handbook page 73.

■ Draw a diagram of something that has a lot of parts.
   You might draw a bicycle, a car, or a new invention!

■ Write words to name the parts.

■ Explain your diagram to your partner.

Main Idea Diagram

📖 Use Handbook page 74.

- What special holiday or event does your family celebrate? Write a sentence about the holiday in the **Main Idea** box.

- Then write a sentence in each **Detail** box to tell what you do to celebrate the holiday.

Main Idea:

Detail:

Detail:

Detail:

Bar Graph

📖 Use Handbook page 76.

- **Read the information in the box.**
- **Use the information to make a bar graph.**

Mr. Davis's Class Read-a-thon

Janell read 10 books.
Jin Ki read 7 books.
Hector read 12 books.
Claire read 6 books.

Mr. Davis's Class Read-a-thon

Pie Graph

📖 Use Handbook page 77.

- Look at the pie graph.
- Read each question.
- Write the answer. Use complete sentences.

Popcorn Sold by Classes at Culver School

1. What percentage of popcorn did Mr. Gomez's class sell?

_____

2. How do you know that Room 2 sold less than Room 4?

_____

3. What percentage of popcorn did Ms. Henderson's class sell?

_____

4. Did Mrs. Romero's class sell more than Mr. Wilson's?

_____

5. Which class sold the most popcorn?

_____

Beginning, Middle, and End Story Map

📖 Use Handbook page 79.

- Read the story on Handbook page 165.

- Finish the story map. Tell what happens in each part of the story.

Title: _Another Saturday Morning_

Beginning

_____

_____

_____

⬇

Middle

1. _____

_____

2. _____

_____

3. _____

_____

4. _____

_____

⬇

End

_____

_____

_____

Name _____   Date _____

Flow Chart

▱ Use Handbook page 87.

■ **Work with a partner.**

■ **Do you know how to make cookies, sew on a button, or play a video game? Talk about what you know how to do.**

■ **Make a flow chart to show the steps.**

Time Line

📖 Use Handbook pages 88–89.

- **Think about important events that have happened at school this year.**

- **Tell about the events on the time line. Use dates to show when the events happened.**

Title: _____

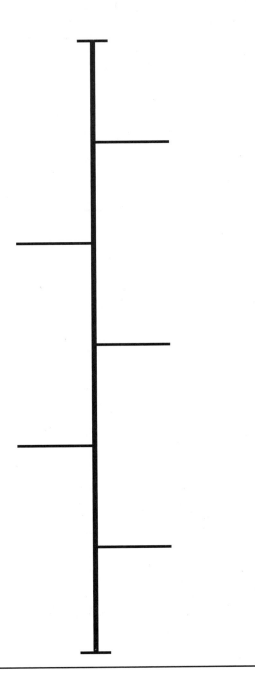

Choosing the Right Words

📖 Use Handbook pages 178–179.

■ **Read the paragraph.**

■ **Rewrite the paragraph. Replace the underlined words with colorful verbs, specific nouns, or comparisons. Add describing words. You might want to use the words in the box.**

as cold as ice	yellow	salty
racket and visor	raced	sweet
faster than lightning	munched on	juicy

    Nikolai picked up his <u>equipment</u> and <u>went</u> to the park for his tennis class. When he got there, Coach hit the ball over the net. Nikolai ran for the ball, but Sara hit it first. She was <u>fast</u>! They played for an hour and then had a snack. Everyone <u>ate</u> popcorn and grapes. Nikolai had a drink of water. It felt <u>cool</u>.

Using a Thesaurus

📖 Use Handbook pages 180–181.

■ Look up each entry word in a thesaurus.

■ Write more synonyms and antonyms for each entry word.

---

clean, *adjective*

synonyms: tidy, *neat, spotless* _____

_____

antonyms: dirty, *filthy, messy,* _____

soiled _____

come, *verb*

synonyms: arrive, _____

_____

antonyms: go, _____

_____

nice, *adjective*

synonyms: good, _____

_____

antonyms: mean, _____

_____

pull, *verb*

synonyms: tug, _____

_____

antonyms: push, _____

_____

warm, *adjective*

synonyms: hot, _____

_____

antonyms: cold, _____

_____

wet, *adjective*

synonyms: soaked, _____

_____

antonyms: dry, _____

_____

Combining Short Sentences

📖 **Use Handbook page 182.**

- **Read the paragraph.**
- **Rewrite the paragraph. Combine the short sentences.**

Paula likes to walk. She walks everywhere. She walks her dog every day. Sometimes she takes him to the park. Sometimes she walks him around her neighborhood. Paula walks to the pool. She goes there in the summer. In the winter, she walks to the frozen lake. She goes there to ice skate. On her autumn walks, Paula loves to look at the colorful trees. She loves to breathe in the cold, fresh air. In the spring, Paula walks. She takes long walks. She can see all the new flowers blooming.

_____

_____

_____

_____

_____

_____

_____

Making Sentences Interesting

📖 Use Handbook pages 182–183.

- Read the paragraph.

- Rewrite the paragraph. Break up sentences that use *and* too many times. Begin some of the sentences in different ways. Use short and long sentences.

    Malcolm loves to swim, and he swims on a swim team and he practices every day of the week for an hour. Malcolm swims four laps of the back stroke on Saturdays while Coach Lee times him. Coach writes the time down in a book so they can keep track of it and Malcolm's time gets faster every week. Coach Lee is very proud of how hard Malcolm works. Malcolm is pleased with the results, too, and he got his first ribbon during a swim meet last week, and it was a red one for second place.

_____

_____

_____

_____

_____

_____

_____

_____

_____

_____

© Hampton-Brown

Writing Good Paragraphs

📖 Use Handbook page 184.

- Read the paragraph.

- Rewrite the paragraph. Break it into smaller paragraphs. Add transition words.

      Last Saturday, my family had our yearly volleyball game. In the morning, Aunt Marie put up the net. My cousin Tonio brought the volleyball. We formed two teams, each one with kids and adults. Uncle Jason yelled, "Are you ready to play?" "We're ready!" everyone screamed. We gathered for a family photo at the park. Mom wanted us to have our picture taken before the sun went down. Chin, our neighbor, came and took the picture. Chin said, "Smile, everybody!"

© Hampton-Brown

Writing a Good Beginning and Conclusion

📖 Use Handbook page 185.

■ **Read the story.**

■ **Rewrite the underlined sentences. Give the story a more interesting beginning and conclusion.**

Mr. Sanderson's class walked out to the baseball field. It was Friday afternoon. Nico's team fanned out across the diamond. Alice's team lined up behind home plate. When Nico pitched the first ball, Alice swung at it as hard as she could. The ball flew high over the kids' heads and landed in the grass. Alice started running to first base, but nobody was looking at her. Everyone was looking over the fence. Three trucks had pulled into the school parking lot. "Jackson's Carnival Rides" was written on the side of each truck. The giant trucks carried the rides for the school carnival.

Beginning: _____

_____

_____

_____

_____

Conclusion: _____

_____

_____

_____

_____

Adding Details

 Use Handbook page 186.

- Talk about the picture with a partner. Make up a story about it.

- Write the story. Use lots of details to make your story interesting to read.

_____

_____

_____

_____

_____

_____

_____

_____

_____

_____

Showing What You Mean

📖 Use Handbook page 187.

- ■ **Read each sentence.**
- ■ **Find the sentence in the box that *shows* exactly what the writer means. Write it in the blank.**

> The audience claps loudly after each performance.
> Andrea spends at least two hours every day to get ready for a concert.
> At Andrea's house, you'll always hear someone singing or playing an instrument.
> "I can listen for hours to works by classical musicians like Bach, Chopin, and Beethoven."
> "There is nothing I would rather do than play the piano."

1. Andrea's family loves music.

At Andrea's house, you'll always hear someone singing or playing an instrument.

2. Andrea's favorite music is classical music.

_____

_____

3. Andrea likes to play the piano.

_____

_____

4. She practices a lot.

_____

_____

5. People like when she performs.

_____

_____

Voice

📖 Use Handbook page 188.

- Read the paragraph about the concert.

- Imagine you were at the concert. Rewrite the paragraph in your own voice.

Last weekend, I went to a Hayriders concert at the County Fair. There were a lot of kids there. When the band came out, the kids screamed. The music was good. They didn't stop for a long time. They played a good song called "Barnyard Rap." Finally, they played a quiet song. I was glad, because they had been really loud all night.

_____

_____

_____

_____

_____

_____

_____

_____

_____

_____

_____

_____

_____

Manuscript Letters

📖 Use Handbook page 211.

- Trace each letter.
- Write the letter two times.

ZB Font Method Copyright © 1996 Zaner-Bloser

Manuscript Letters

Use Handbook page 211.

- Trace each letter.
- Write the letter two times.

ZB Font Method Copyright © 1996 Zaner-Bloser

© Hampton-Brown

Cursive Letters

📖 Use Handbook page 215.

- Trace each letter.
- Write the letter two times.

ZB Font Method Copyright © 1996 Zaner-Bloser

Cursive Letters

📖 **Use Handbook page 215.**

- **Trace each letter.**
- **Write the letter two times.**

ZB Font Method Copyright © 1996 Zaner-Bloser

© Hampton-Brown

Spelling Words with *-ed, -ing, -er, -est*

📖 Use Handbook pages 222–223.

- Read the message.
- Add the ending to the missing word. Write the word in the blank.

```
┌─────────────────────────────────────────────────────────────┐
│ □  ═══════════  ⊡  The biggest mistake!  ══════════  ⊟▯▮│
├─────────────────────────────────────────────────────────────┤
│   To:   │ Kim Chang                          │      ⊟➡      │
│         └────────────────────────────────────┘               │
│ Subject:│ The biggest mistake!               │     Send      │
│         └────────────────────────────────────┘               │
├─────────────────────────────────────────────────────────────┤
│                                                               │
│   Dear Kim,                                                   │
│                                                               │
│   I have the  *funniest*  story. Last night, I _____ to make cookies.
│              **1. funny + est**              **2. try + ed**  │
│                                                               │
│   I _____ the eggs and _____ them to the other ingredients.
│      **3. crack + ed**        **4. add + ed**                 │
│                                                               │
│   Then I _____ the cookies. After they cooled, I ate one. It was the
│           **5. bake + ed**                                    │
│                                                               │
│   _____ thing I had ever _____! I had used salt instead of
│   **6. salty + est**          **7. taste + ed**               │
│                                                               │
│   sugar! Now I am _____ again. I am _____ more cookies.
│                   **8. try + ing**        **9. bake + ing**   │
│                                                               │
│   I feel much _____ this time.                           │
│               **10. wise + er**                               │
│                                                               │
│                                                               │
│   Your friend,                                                │
│                                                               │
│   Leti                                                        │
│                                                               │
└─────────────────────────────────────────────────────────────┘
```

© Hampton-Brown

Spelling Words with Prefixes and Suffixes

📖 Use Handbook pages 224–225.

- Look at each picture. Read the sentences.
- Add the prefix or suffix to the missing word. Write the word in the blank.

1. Sara's research is ____incomplete____.
   in + complete

2. She will _____ the article in her
   re + read

   encyclopedia.

3. She will be _____ as she takes notes.
   care + ful

4. Ben _____ likes to read.
   real + ly

5. He finds a _____ book in the library.
   wonder + ful

6. It is full of tales about an _____ boy.
   adventure + ous

7. Marvin walked _____ in his old shoes.
   uncomfortable + ly

8. _____, he got new shoes for his birthday.
   Lucky + ly

9. He was _____ when he tried them on.
   joy + ous

Spelling Plurals

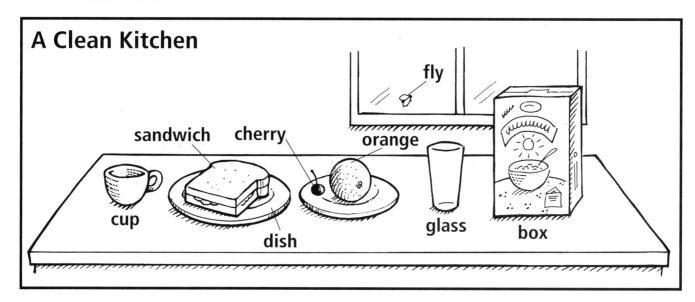

Use Handbook page 226.

- Read each word in the top picture.

- Look at the bottom picture. Write the plural of each word.

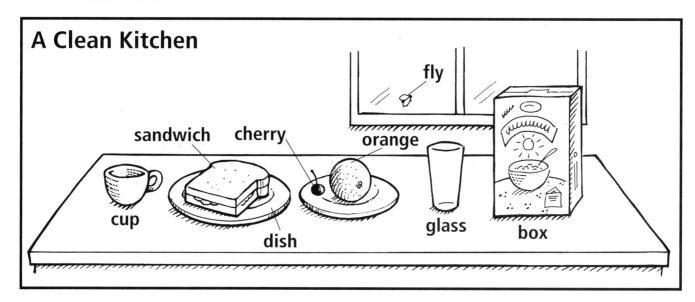

A Clean Kitchen

fly

sandwich   cherry   orange

cup   dish   glass   box

A Messy Kitchen!

1.   2.   3.   4.   5.   6.   7.   8.

1. _cups_____   4. _____   7. _____

2. _____   5. _____   8. _____

3. _____   6. _____

Spelling Long Words

 Use Handbook page 227.

■ **Match the syllables. Draw a line to connect them.**

■ **Write the complete words below the picture.**

First Syllable	Second Syllable
1. sum	kle
2. lit	den
3. gar	cross
4. back	mer
5. a	shine
6. rab	tle
7. spar	yard
8. sun	bit

1. *summer* _____   **5.** _____

2. _____   **6.** _____

3. _____   **7.** _____

4. _____   **8.** _____

Spelling Words That Sound Alike

📖 Use Handbook pages 228–229.

- Read each sentence.
- Write the correct word in the blank.

1. Emma wanted some new _____.

clothes / close

2. She needed something to _____ to

where / wear

a birthday party.

3. She went shopping for a _____ dress.

knew / new

4. She said to the clerk, "I _____ you are having a sale."

heard / herd

5. The clerk showed Emma a white dress with _____ stripes.

red / read

6. She showed Emma a blue dress, _____.

two / too / to

7. " _____ both so pretty!" Emma said.

There / They're / Their

8. She couldn't decide _____ to buy the striped dress or the blue dress.

weather / whether

9. "Have you made up _____ mind?" the clerk asked.

your / you're

10. "I'll take the striped one," Emma said. " _____ my favorite."

Its / It's

Kinds of Sentences

📖 **Use Handbook page 232.**

- **Read each sentence.**
- **Write an ending from the box to finish each kind of sentence.**

us about him.	is he holding?
park ranger.	new statue.
John Henry?	hear what he did!
so strong!	a hammer.

· JOHN HENRY ·

1. statement   Here is a *new statue.* _____

2. question   Who is _____

3. command   Ask the _____

4. exclamation   The man looks _____

5. question   What _____

6. statement   It looks like _____

7. command   Please tell _____

8. exclamation   I can't wait to _____

Kinds of Sentences

Use Handbook page 233.

- Read each sentence.
- Change the sentence into a question.
  Write the question.

1. We are going to see John Henry's statue.

   Are we going to see John Henry's statue?

2. Mark wants to see the statue, too.

   _____

3. Adela is going with him.

   _____

4. The new statue is huge.

   _____

5. Mark has read about John Henry.

   _____

6. Adela wants to read about John Henry and Pecos Bill.

   _____

7. She would enjoy reading the tall tales.

   _____

8. Adela could read about the characters in Mark's book.

   _____

9. The park will get a statue of Pecos Bill, too.

   _____

10. Adela and Mark should come back to see the Pecos Bill statue.

    _____

Kinds of Sentences

📖 Use Handbook page 233.

- ■ **Read each statement.**
- ■ **Add a question to the end.**
  Write the question.
- ■ **Can your partner answer each question?**

1. You do know about John Henry.

You do know about John Henry,
don't you?

2. John Henry is a folk hero.

_____

_____

3. He worked on the railroads in West Virginia.

_____

_____

4. John Henry was a powerful man.

_____

5. He could pound steel into rock.

_____

6. He raced a steam drill.

_____

7. The steam drill couldn't beat him.

_____

8. John Henry showed that a man could dig faster than a machine.

_____

_____

Kinds of Sentences

📖 Use Handbook page 234.

- Look at the picture.
- Write questions about the picture.
- Read your questions to a partner. Can your partner answer them?

1. Who *is working on the railroad?* _____

2. Where _____

3. Why _____

4. How many _____

5. When _____

6. How _____

7. Which _____

8. What _____

Kinds of Sentences

📖 Use Handbook page 235.

- **Work with a partner. Read the story about Paul Bunyan on Handbook page 146.**

- **Read each question. Write the answer. Use negative words.**

Negative Words	
nowhere	nobody
never	no
no one	none
not	nothing

1. Before Paul built the bunkhouses, did his men have somewhere to sleep? *Before Paul built the bunkhouses, his men had nowhere to sleep.*

2. Were the new bunkhouses small? _____

_____

3. Did anybody walk up to bed? _____

_____

4. Did anyone walk down to breakfast? _____

_____

5. Could any of the cooks flip flapjacks fast enough? _____

_____

6. Did the men ever run out of syrup for their flapjacks? _____

_____

7. Was anything left of the hills when the men leveled the Great Plains? _____

_____

8. Were there any trees left after the men shaved the slopes of the Rocky Mountains? _____

_____

Subject and Predicate

📖 Use Handbook pages 236–237.

- ■ **Work with a partner.**

- ■ **Look at the picture. Talk about the tall tale characters.**

- ■ **Write a subject or a predicate to finish each sentence.**

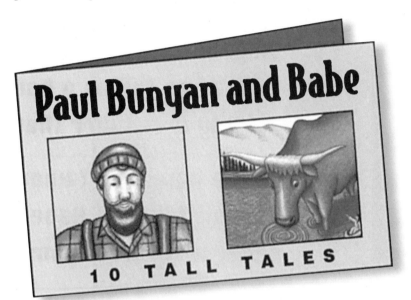

1. _____Danny and Ellen_____ love to read tall tales.

2. _____ is their favorite tall tale character.

3. Paul _____ .

4. He _____ .

5. Paul's best friend _____ .

6. _____ is a big, blue ox.

7. _____ helped Paul with his work.

8. Babe _____ .

9. _____ made paths through the mountains.

10. Babe and Paul _____ .

Compound Sentences

📖 **Use Handbook page 238.**

- **Read the story.**

- **Write *and, but,* or *or* to join the two parts of each compound sentence. Use the correct punctuation.**

When Pecos Bill was a baby, he was traveling

West with his family, _but_ he fell out of the
                        1

wagon. Pecos fell into a river_____ a coyote
                                   2

saved him. "I could give him back to the humans_____ I could
                                                   3

raise him as my own," she thought. The coyote took the baby

to her den_____ Pecos Bill learned how to live like a coyote.
           4

One day, Cowboy Hank was out riding on the range_____ his
                                                   5

horse almost stepped on Pecos Bill. Pecos was asleep_____ Hank woke
                                                       6

him up. Hank told Pecos that he was a human_____ Pecos believed he
                                              7

was a coyote. Hank said, "I can show you how to be a cowboy_____
                                                             8

you can stay with the coyotes."

Pecos Bill decided to be a cowboy_____ Hank helped him start
                                   9

a ranch. Soon Pecos had gathered every steer in Texas_____ people
                                                        10

talked about how he was the greatest cowboy in the country.

Singular and Plural Nouns

📖 Use Handbook page 240.

bay	box	coach	butterfly	Sunday	roof
story					cave
man					beach
child					woman
leaf					city
island					person
BEGIN		**THE END**	knife	house	cliff

How to Play
The Noun Game

1. Play with a partner.
2. Use an eraser or small object as your game piece. Use a coin to show how many spaces to move.

   Heads = 1 space

   Tails = 2 spaces

3. Read the singular noun.
4. Say the plural noun. Write it on a sheet of paper.
5. The first one to reach THE END wins.

Singular and Plural Nouns

📖 Use Handbook pages 240–241.

■ Read the sentence.

■ Write the word in dark print in the blank. Make the word plural if you need to.

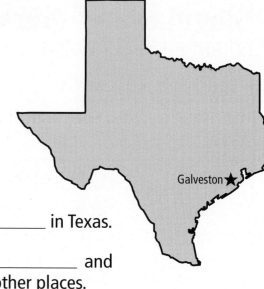
Galveston ★

city   1. Galveston is one of the most

important _____ *cities* _____ in Texas.

rice   2. From this port, _____ and other products are shipped to other places.

sugar   3. Bananas, _____, and automobiles are shipped in.

tea   4. Galveston produces _____ and frozen seafood.

visitor   5. This city also gets a lot of _____ .

beach   6. They like to visit the many _____ along the coast.

heat   7. The beach is a great place to go in the summer

_____ .

water   8. The weather is perfect for swimming in the

_____ .

football 9. People also like to play _____ in the city parks.

child   10. In April, _____ can go to a special festival.

kite   11. At the festival, they can fly all kinds of _____ .

money   12. People can have fun in Galveston without spending

a lot of _____ .

Words That Signal Nouns

Use Handbook page 242.

- **Read the paragraphs.**

- **Write the word that identifies the noun.**
  Use *a, the, some,* or *an.*

Luisa loves __*the*__ ocean. She read _____ interesting article
                1   2

about it. There is _____ underwater garden 100 miles off the coast
                      3

of Galveston. It is called _____ Flower Garden National Marine
                              4

Sanctuary. _____ marine sanctuary is a place where the fish
              5

and _____ ocean's plants are protected.
        6

_____ kinds of fish that live in the sanctuary are Caribbean reef fish.
    7

The manta ray is _____ animal that lives there, too. The underwater
                    8

garden is also _____ good home for turtles. All the animals swim
                  9

around _____ coral reefs and sand flats.
          10

Luisa wants to become _____ marine researcher.
                          11

She wants to study _____ more places like the
                      12

Flower Garden Marine Sanctuary.

Words That Signal Nouns

📖 Use Handbook page 242.

- ■ Read each sentence.
- ■ Write the word *a*, *the*, *some*, or *an* to finish the sentence.

1. My family takes _____a_____ vacation every year.

2. I think Stewart Beach on Galveston Island is _____ great place to go.

3. We go there in _____ summer.

4. We never forget to take _____ sunscreen.

5. Mom always brings _____ snacks, too.

6. It only takes _____ hour to get there.

7. At the beach, my brother and I always build _____ sandcastles.

8. Sometimes we toss _____ ball back and forth.

9. Then we swim in _____ ocean.

10. My mom sits under _____ umbrella.

11. She enjoys reading _____ good book.

12. Everyone always has _____ good time.

Words That Signal Nouns

📖 Use Handbook page 243.

- **Read each sentence.**
- **Choose the correct word below the line.**
- **Write the word in the blank.**

1. "Galveston has great stores," said Mom. "Let's

   go in _____*that*_____ store across the street."

        this / that

2. "_____ store is great," I told the

  Those / This

   clerk. "Do you have tennis shoes?"

3. "Yes, we do. _____ shoes over by the door are

      This / Those

   our latest styles."

4. "I would like to try on _____ pair on the bottom shelf."

      that / these

5. "What about _____ pair?" asked Mom.

     these / this

6. "_____ shoes fit perfectly," I said.

  This / These

7. "Can I get some socks from _____ rack in the back?"

      that / those

8. "Sure," said Mom. "_____ socks look just right

     Those / This

   for tennis, too."

Possessive Nouns

📖 **Use Handbook page 244.**

- Read each sentence.
- Add an apostrophe (') and an *s* to the word in dark print to show if there is one owner or more than one owner.
- Write the word in the blank.

TEXAS

Galveston ★

Galveston 1. When you go to _____*Galveston's*_____ shops, you can find lots of souvenirs.

friend 2. My three _____ favorite souvenirs are T-shirts.

shirt 3. There are different designs on the _____ fronts.

museum 4. Many shirts have a _____ name on them.

boy 5. Both _____ shirts say "Flight Museum."

girl 6. The _____ shirt says "Galveston Spring Fest."

father 7. My _____ caps are from Galveston, too.

cap 8. The _____ fronts say "Joe's Cafe."

restaurant 9. Dad really likes that _____ food!

mom 10. My _____ favorite souvenirs are hats.

shop 11. We look in all the _____ windows until we find a hat with a ribbon on it.

hat 12. Her _____ ribbon is a beautiful green color.

Possessive Nouns

📖 Use Handbook page 244.

- ■ **Read each sentence.**
- ■ **Choose the correct word from below the line.**
- ■ **Write the word in the blank.**

1. On Saturday _____*Michael's*_____ uncle asked Michael and Paul
                Michael's / Michaels'
   what they wanted to see.

2. The boys looked in the _____ brochure.
                    hotel's / hotels'

3. The _____ choice was the Tall Ship *Elissa*.
           boy's / boys'

4. They went to see the ship at _____ dock.
                  Galveston's / Galvestons'

5. Uncle Pete said, "Imagine traveling over an _____
                              ocean's / oceans'
   waves without a motor."

6. "It took several sailors to raise that _____ sails."
                          ship's / ships'

7. "The _____ jobs must have been hard."
           sailor's / sailors'

8. "Most of the _____ decks were made of hard wood."
             ship's / ships'

9. "The _____ surface must have been uncomfortable to sleep on!"
           deck's / decks'

10. The boys took lots of pictures with Uncle _____ camera.
                                 Pete's / Petes'

Using Nouns in Writing

📖 Use Handbook page 245.

- ■ **Read the paragraph. Look at the underlined words.**

- ■ **Rewrite the paragraph. Replace the underlined words with specific nouns.**

     In <u>the neighborhood</u>, everyone likes to eat out. We go to <u>the restaurant</u>. There you can get good food for lunch or dinner. For lunch, I like to eat <u>a sandwich</u>. I also order a large <u>drink</u>. If we go there for dinner, I usually get <u>pasta</u>. Sometimes I have <u>a vegetable</u>, too. For dessert, you can choose from several <u>things</u>. I always save room for <u>dessert</u> because it's so good!

_____

_____

_____

_____

_____

_____

_____

_____

_____

_____

_____

_____

Pronouns

📖 **Use Handbook pages 246–247.**

■ **Read the sentences.**

■ **Mark the pronoun that goes in each blank.**

■ **Write the pronoun on the line next to the sentence.**

Lisa   Tom   Joey

Coach Brown

1. Today is Saturday. _____ is the day we play soccer.
   ○ You   ● It   ○ I
   _____It_____

2. Mr. Brown blows the whistle. _____ is our soccer coach.
   ○ She   ○ He   ○ It
   _____

3. Joey is the goalie. _____ gets into position.
   ○ He   ○ You   ○ I
   _____

4. The Rangers run out to the field. _____ are ready for the kick.
   ○ It   ○ They   ○ You
   _____

5. "Tom, are _____ ready to receive the ball?" asks Lisa.
   ○ you   ○ I   ○ it
   _____

6. "Yes, _____ am!" says Tom.
   ○ I   ○ you   ○ he
   _____

7. Lisa runs. _____ kicks the ball to Tom.
   ○ I   ○ They   ○ She
   _____

8. "Hooray!" _____ all cheer when Tom kicks the ball into the net.
   ○ He   ○ It   ○ We
   _____

© Hampton-Brown

Pronouns

📖 Use Handbook page 248.

- **Read the paragraphs. Look at the underlined words.**

- **Rewrite the paragraphs. Use pronouns to take the place of the underlined words.**

Tom

Lisa

Coach Brown

Last Saturday was the third game of the season. When Tom and Lisa got to the field it started to sprinkle. Coach told Tom and Lisa to try to play anyway. "A little rain shouldn't bother all the Bobcats," Coach told Lisa.

So Lisa ran out to the field. The rain was falling harder. Tom tried to kick the ball to Lisa but slipped on the wet grass. The player next to Tom slipped, too. Soon everyone was laughing. The game was cancelled, but the players on both teams all had a great time!

_____

_____

_____

_____

_____

_____

_____

_____

_____

_____

_____

Pronouns

Use Handbook page 249.

- Read each sentence.
- Choose the correct word below the line.
- Write the word in the blank.

1. Coach was cleaning out _____*our*_____ bag of soccer equipment.
   our / ours

2. "Whose shin guards are these?" he asked.

   "Oh, those are _____," said Tom.
   my / mine

   Tom

3. "What about this cap? Is it _____, Juan?"
   your / yours

   Juan

4. "No," said Juan. "I think it's Mary's. _____ cap is yellow."
   Her / Hers

   Jasmine

5. "Jasmine, is this your shoe?"

   "No, it must be Juan's. He lost _____," she said.
   his / hers

6. "Does this goalie mask belong to the Eagles? I think it's _____,"
   their / theirs
   said Tom.

7. "Finally, here's _____ whistle!" said Coach.
   my / mine

   Coach Brown

8. "Did the dog lose _____ cap?"
   its / it's

9. "Well, _____ not lost anymore."
   its / it's

   Nuff

10. "_____ here, too."
    Its / It's

© Hampton-Brown

Pronouns

📖 Use Handbook page 250.

- Read what Jasmine and her mother are saying.

- Use words from the box to finish their sentences. Write the words in the blanks.

everyone	something	everybody	somebody
anything	someone	everything	anyone

"How was the party after the game?" asked Mom.

" ___Everything___ was great," said Jasmine.
              1

"Did the whole team go? Was _____ there?"
                                                    2

" _____ on the team came," answered Jasmine.
         3

"We were so happy that we won _____."
                                            4

"Did you have _____ to eat?"
                      5

"Yes, we did. I don't know who made the oatmeal cookies,

but _____ is a good cook. They were delicious!"
         6

"Did _____ bring a camera?"
              7

" _____ did, but I'm not sure who. I can't wait
         8

to see the pictures!"

© Hampton-Brown

Using Pronouns in Writing

📖 Use Handbook page 251.

- Read the letter. Look at the underlined nouns.

- Rewrite the paragraphs in the letter. Replace each underlined noun with a pronoun from the box.

Pronouns			
he	she	it	they
his	him	their	them

575 Hannon St.
Dallas, TX 75201
September 12, 2003

Dear Joseph,

How's soccer? I got a letter from Tom. Tom said that the Bobcats are playing the Eagles next week. The Eagles will be hard to beat.

I remember when we played against the Eagles. The Eagles' goalie is really good. Mike is Mike's name. It's hard to get a ball past Mike. There's also a player named Melissa. Melissa is a fast runner!

Good luck in your game. I hope you win the game!

Your pal,
Ramon

_____

_____

_____

_____

_____

_____

Using Adjectives to Describe

📖 Use Handbook page 252.

- **Look at the picture.**
- **Read each sentence.**
- **Write a word from the chart to finish the sentence.**

What Something Is Like		Which One
wet	round	first
smooth	long	third
croaking	strong	second
delicious		

1. Many frogs live in the _____ wet _____ rain forest.

2. The frogs have _____ skin.

3. Their eyes are big and _____.

4. The _____ frog is jumping to a different branch.

5. The _____ frog is catching a bug.

6. The frog uses its _____ tongue to catch it.

7. A bug tastes _____ to a frog.

8. The _____ frog is sleeping.

9. It hangs onto the branch with its _____ toes.

10. I wonder if the frog makes a _____ sound when it sleeps!

Using Adjectives to Describe

📖 Use Handbook page 253.

- **Look at the picture.**
- **Read each sentence.**
- **Write a word from the box to finish the sentence.**

not any	many	three	nine
not much	any	several	much

1. These ___*three*___ big caimans look like alligators.

2. They have _____ teeth!

3. When they float, _____ of their body shows.

4. It is amazing that they swallow hardly _____ water.

5. A baby caiman is just eight or _____ inches long.

6. Caimans grow up to be _____ bigger!

7. Caimans eat _____ kinds of animals.

8. No wonder there are _____ monkeys nearby!

Using Adjectives to Compare

📖 Use Handbook pages 254–255.

- **Look at the pictures.**
- **Read each sentence. Write the correct word in the blank.**

jaguar

puma

ocelot

1. The jaguar is the _____*largest*_____ wild cat in the Americas.
        larger / largest

2. It is also the _____ powerful of the cats.
        more / most

3. With its golden or brownish yellow spots, the jaguar is _____
colorful than the puma.   more / most

4. The ocelot has _____ spots, too.
        more / some

5. The ocelot and the puma are _____ climbers than the jaguar.
        better / best

6. The ocelot and the jaguar are _____ swimmers.
        good / best

7. An adult jaguar usually weighs _____ than a puma.
        more / most

8. The puma is _____ than a jaguar.
        thinner / thinnest

9. The ocelot weighs the _____ amount of all.
        less / least

10. It's the _____ wild cat.
        smaller / smallest

© Hampton-Brown

Using Adjectives in Writing

Use Handbook page 257.

- Talk about the picture with a partner.
- Write sentences to tell about the plants and animals. Use lots of adjectives.

tree

quetzal

butterflies

jaguar

hummingbirds

frog

lily pads

snake

grass

_____

_____

_____

_____

_____

_____

_____

_____

_____

© Hampton-Brown

Action Verbs

📖 Use Handbook page 258.

■ **Read each sentence.**

■ **Write the correct verb from the box.**

1. I _____ *like* _____ autumn.

2. At that time of year, the temperature _____ to 45 degrees.

3. The leaves _____ different colors.

4. They _____ off the trees.

5. The wind _____ the leaves all around.

6. I _____ outside in the cool, crisp air.

| like |
| turn |
| drops |
| fall |
| blows |
| play |

7. In autumn, my school _____ again.

8. Dad _____ me up early.

9. My sister and I _____ breakfast.

10. Then we _____ on the bus.

11. At school I _____ friends that I haven't seen all summer.

12. We all _____ to new classrooms with new teachers.

| wakes |
| ride |
| go |
| see |
| eat |
| starts |

Linking Verbs

📖 Use Handbook page 258.

- ■ **Read each sentence.**
- ■ **Choose the correct verb below the line. Write the verb in the blank.**

1. I _____*am*_____ a cloud watcher.
        am / is

2. Look! There _____ some fluffy, white clouds.
              is / are

3. One cloud _____ in the shape of a dragon!
           is / are

4. Yesterday there _____ gray rain clouds in the sky.
           was / were

5. After it rained, there _____ a beautiful rainbow.
           was / were

6. Heavy, dark clouds _____ in the sky last week.
           was / were

7. I knew then that snow _____ on its way.
           was / were

8. Now you know why clouds _____ interesting to watch.
           is / are

9. They _____ clues that tell what the weather will be like.
        is / are

10. I _____ curious about what the clouds will tell me
        am / is

about the weather tomorrow.

Helping Verbs

📖 Use Handbook page 259.

■ Read each sentence.

■ Write the correct verb from the box.

■ Circle the helping verb in each answer.

1. Early this morning, the sun ____(was) shining____ .

2. By 11 a.m., however, the weather _____ .

3. Blankets of gray clouds _____ the sun.

4. The temperature _____ lower.

5. I thought it _____ .

6. At 2 p.m., snowflakes _____ to fall.

| did start |
| had changed |
| was shining |
| were blocking |
| might snow |
| had dropped |

7. We _____ it snow from the window.

8. The snow _____ the ground.

9. "We _____ outside to play," I said to my sister.

10. "We _____ a snow castle!"

11. My sister _____ her coat already.

12. She _____ out the door.

| can build |
| was running |
| were watching |
| should go |
| had grabbed |
| was covering |

© Hampton-Brown

Contractions with Verbs

📖 Use Handbook page 260.

- **Read the paragraph. Look at the underlined words.**

- **Rewrite the paragraph. Replace the underlined words with contractions.**

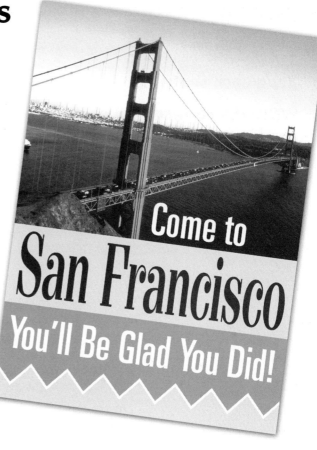

Come to
San Francisco
You'll Be Glad You Did!

    <u>Where is</u> the best place to visit? <u>I would</u> say San Francisco. <u>I have</u> been there several times. You <u>should not</u> have to drive anywhere because you can ride on a cable car or on a bus. <u>You will</u> love walking down the steep, crooked streets! <u>Do not</u> miss the Golden Gate Bridge! You <u>cannot</u> leave without seeing it. The weather <u>is not</u> too cold, but take a jacket. <u>It is</u> cool and sometimes foggy at night. You <u>have not</u> had fun until <u>you have</u> been to San Francisco!

_____

_____

_____

_____

_____

_____

_____

_____

Present-Tense Verbs

 Use Handbook page 261.

- Read each sentence.
- Write the correct form of the verb in the blank.

enjoy **1.** In our neighborhood, we ____*enjoy*____ all kinds of weather.

love **2.** Eric _____ the rain.

see **3.** He _____ it pour down from his window.

want **4.** Anna _____ to catch the rain in a bucket so she can measure it.

like **5.** I _____ the winter months.

freeze **6.** The lake _____ then.

skate **7.** My friend and I _____ on the frozen lake.

ride **8.** In the spring, all the kids _____ their bikes.

ask **9.** Sometimes my dad _____, "Can I go with you?"

swim **10.** During hot weather, Juan _____ every day.

sell **11.** Sue and Joli are smart! They _____ us lemonade on hot days.

taste **12.** The cool lemonade _____ great!

Present-Tense Verbs

📖 **Use Handbook page 261.**

swim	run	hold
walk	wear	look
sled	bark	

■ **Look at each picture. Read the sentences.**

■ **Choose a verb from the box to tell what the people are doing. Write the correct form of the verb in the blank.**

1. Manuel ___swims___ in the pool.

2. He _____ goggles on his face.

5. Mia and her grandmother _____ in the rain.

6. They _____ umbrellas.

3. Vi _____ across a field.

4. She _____ at her kite.

7. Jamal _____ down the hill.

8. His dog _____ happily.

Past-Tense Verbs

📖 **Use Handbook page 262.**

- **Read each question.**
- **Add _–ed_ to the underlined verb to make it tell about the past.**
- **Use the past-tense verb to finish the answer.**

1. Did you <u>watch</u> the weather report last night?

   Yes, we _watched the weather report last night._

2. Did the scientists <u>gather</u> information for it?

   Yes, the scientists _____

3. Did they <u>study</u> the weather patterns?

   Yes, they _____

4. Did they <u>use</u> many tools?

   Yes, they _____

5. Did the balloons <u>stay</u> in the air to measure the wind speeds?

   Yes, the balloons _____

   _____

6. Did the weather satellites <u>snap</u> pictures of the clouds?

   Yes, the weather satellites _____

   _____

7. Did the tools <u>measure</u> wind, air, and temperature?

   Yes, the tools _____

8. Did the reporter <u>predict</u> the weather?

   Yes, the reporter _____

Past-Tense Verbs

📖 Use Handbook page 263.

- **Read the paragraph. Look at the underlined words.**

- **Rewrite the paragraph to make it tell about an action that happened in the past.**

How <u>do</u> some people predict the weather? Everyday things and animals <u>give</u> them clues. Some people <u>say</u> to look at the color of the sky. A dark, cloudy sky <u>brings</u> rain or snow. A clear, blue sky <u>is</u> a sign of fair weather ahead. Other people <u>find</u> a clue from the groundhog. If the groundhog <u>sees</u> its shadow, there'd be six more weeks of winter. Spring <u>begins</u> if the groundhog could not see its shadow. On the seacoast, people <u>keep</u> seaweed hanging near their houses. The seaweed <u>gets</u> dry in clear weather. A clump of wool <u>holds</u> moisture in rainy weather. During stormy weather, some animals <u>hide</u> in caves. Other animals <u>go</u> underground. There <u>are</u> clues everywhere!

_____

_____

_____

_____

_____

_____

_____

_____

_____

_____

Name _____ Date _____

Future-Tense Verbs

📖 Use Handbook page 264.

■ **What is the boy going to do in the future?**

■ **Choose words from the box to finish each sentence.**

Rain Gauge

rain

top of soda bottle used as funnel

shampoo bottle without top

marks for water levels

soda bottle

1. Tomorrow, Tran _____*will make*_____ a rain gauge.

2. He _____ an old plastic bottle.

3. The marks on the bottle _____ different water levels.

4. "I _____ the gauge outside," said Tran.

5. "The rain _____ into the gauge."

6. "I _____ at the water level every morning."

7. "I _____ the number of inches to see how much rain falls."

8. "The gauge _____, though, if it doesn't rain!"

will make
am going to put
will fall
will look
is going to use
are going to show
will write
won't work

Present-Perfect Tense

📖 Use Handbook pages 265–266.

- Read each sentence.
- Write the verb in the blank. Use the present-perfect tense.

see   1. I ____ *have seen* ____ many changes in our garden.

be   2. The weather _____ very hot and dry.

have 3. We _____ no rain for a long time.

stop 4. Most of the flowers _____ growing.

harden 5. The soil _____.

find 6. We _____ new ways to make our garden look nice.

create 7. My mother _____ a pretty rock garden.

plant 8. My father _____ a tall cactus.

paint 9. We _____ a rainbow on our fence.

begin 10. Today I saw a rain cloud! I _____ to hope that the rain will return.

Past-Perfect Tense

📖 Use Handbook pages 265 and 267.

- ■ **Read the paragraph.**
- ■ **Write each verb in the blank.**
  Use the past-perfect tense.

The morning sky ___*had looked*___ sunny, so my brother Lee decided
                    1. look

to go on a bike ride. He _____ for a mile before raindrops
                          2. ride

began to fall. He felt scared because dark clouds _____ the
                                                    3. fill

sky. The wind _____ strong. Lee began to wish that he
               4. grow

_____ home! By the time Lee reached our street, the rain
5. stay

_____ to fall very hard. I ran out with an umbrella because
6. start

I _____ him coming up the street. He was already soaked
  7. see

because he _____ caught in the storm. We were glad to see
            8. get

him. We _____ where he was! We _____
        9. wonder   **10. be**

very worried about him.

Using Verbs in Writing

📖 Use Handbook page 268.

■ **Read the story. Look at the underlined words.**

■ **Rewrite the story. Replace the underlined words with colorful verbs. You may want to use words from the box.**

Colorful Verbs	
flashed	shouted
grabbed	stared
hurried	jumped
raced	roared
pounded	slammed

One morning, I <u>got</u> out of bed. "What's that noise?" I <u>said</u>. I <u>got</u> my slippers. Then I <u>went</u> to the window. I <u>looked</u> outside. Lightning <u>was</u> in the sky. Then the thunder <u>came</u>. After that, balls of hail <u>were</u> against the house. I <u>put</u> the window down just in time! I <u>moved</u> back into my warm, cozy bed.

_____

_____

_____

_____

_____

_____

_____

Adverbs

📖 Use Handbook page 269.

- Read each sentence.
- Write the correct adverb from the box to finish each sentence.

1. Roger went to the new gym ___*yesterday*___ .

2. It's nice _____ the gym.

3. Roger goes there _____ to practice.

4. He jumped _____ to reach the rings.

5. He swung _____ back and forth on the rings.

6. Roger's arms are _____ strong.

slowly
inside
really
yesterday
high
often

---

7. Then Roger swung back and forth _____ .

8. He brought his legs _____ and flipped all the way around!

9. He let go and flew _____ the rings.

10. He landed _____ on the soft mat.

11. Roger is a _____ good gymnast.

12. He _____ performs well.

very
always
perfectly
up
off
more quickly

© Hampton-Brown

Using Adverbs to Compare

📖 Use Handbook page 270.

- **Read each sentence.**

- **Choose the correct word below the line.
  Write the word in the blank.**

1. This floor show is _____*longer*_____
   than last year's.   longer / longest

2. Look! Ciara is tumbling

   _____ than Lu.
        faster / fastest

3. Of all the performers, Mariah walks _____ gracefully
   across the balance beam.   more / most

4. Of all the gymnasts I know, Beto loses his balance on the high beam

   the _____ frequently.
          less / least

5. He is also _____ careful than Jason on the rings.
                more / most

6. Lu finishes the floor exercise _____ of all the competitors.
                                     faster / fastest

7. The coaches look _____ worried today than they
   did yesterday.   less / least

8. The judges are the _____ I have ever met.
                        friendlier / friendliest

9. The audience is clapping _____ loudly than they
   ever have before.   more / most

10. This is the _____ exciting performance I have ever seen!
                    more / most

© Hampton-Brown

Name _____ Date _____

Using Adverbs in Writing

📖 Use Handbook page 271.

- **Read the letter.**
- **Write adverbs from the box.**

always	really
inside	highest
more carefully	often
well	perfectly

683 Willow Rd.
Los Angeles, CA 90015
March 6, 2003

Dear Bill,

Our gymnastic team did very _____**well**_____ in
                                    1
the competition last week. It was held _____
                                              2
the new gym on Oak Street.

It was _____ exciting to see Ciara
              3
perform. She walked _____ across the beam
                          4
than anyone else. Beto jumped the _____ of
                                        5
all the gymnasts. Jason didn't make any mistakes during

his routine. He tumbled _____.
                              6

I know you don't travel _____, but
                              7
maybe you'll come to see us. I _____ want
                                    8
to show off my team! I hope to see you soon.

Your friend,

Coach Raphael

Prepositions

📖 **Use Handbook page 272.**

- **Look at the picture.**
- **Read each sentence.**
- **Write a word from the box to tell where things are.**

1. The children's kites are _____*in*_____ the sky.

2. The kites are _____ the children's heads.

3. The girl's kite is _____ the boy's kite and a tree.

4. Her kite is right _____ the tree.

5. Oh no! It's going to crash _____ the tree!

6. There's a kite already _____ a branch.

7. That kite's tail is wrapped _____ the branch.

8. Will someone get the kite's tail _____ the branch?

above
on
next to
between
off
in
into
around

© Hampton-Brown

Prepositions

📖 Use Handbook page 272.

- Read each sentence.
- Mark the preposition that goes in the sentence.
- Write the preposition on the line next to the sentence.

1. There is going to be a Kite Festival _____ April 24. _____*on*_____
   - ● on   ○ in   ○ from

2. It's going to be held _____ 10 a.m. to 7 p.m. _____
   - ○ from   ○ until   ○ for

3. Children should sign up for the kite-flying contest _____ noon. _____
   - ○ in   ○ before   ○ on

4. There will be lots of games to play _____ the day, too. _____
   - ○ from   ○ to   ○ during

5. The kite-flying contest will be held _____ 2 p.m. _____
   - ○ in   ○ after   ○ from

6. Later _____ the afternoon there will be a kite-making workshop. _____
   - ○ in   ○ on   ○ without

7. Awards will be given out from 3:30 p.m. _____ 4:30 p.m. _____
   - ○ during   ○ to   ○ with

8. When the awards are over, there'll be a picnic that will last _____ dark. _____
   - ○ until   ○ from   ○ on

Using Prepositions in Writing

📖 Use Handbook page 273.

- Read the story.

- Add details to the story.
  Use prepositional phrases
  from the boxes.

_____*In August*_____, Dad and I went to
                1

Chicago. It was my first trip _____.
                                        2

We got to the airport _____ in the
                                3

morning. We went _____ and
                            4

showed our tickets. Then we walked

_____ to our gate.
          5

| on an airplane |
| to the counter |
| at 10 o'clock |
| In August |
| down a hallway |

When we got on the airplane, we found two seats

_____. We pushed our small
          6

suitcases _____ and sat down.
                    7

We buckled our seat belts _____.
                                      8

Soon the airplane lifted _____.
                                    9

We flew for an hour and landed in Chicago

_____.
          10

| under the seats |
| off the ground |
| around our laps |
| next to each other |
| before noon |

Using Conjunctions in Writing

📖 Use Handbook page 275.

- ■ **Read the paragraph.**

- ■ **Rewrite the paragraph. Use a comma and the conjunction** *and, but,* **or** *or* **to join the short sentences.**

I love sports. Basketball is my favorite.
I like the Coyotes. I like the Falcons better.
Last Saturday I went to a Falcons–Coyotes
game. I sat with the Falcons' fans.

It was the last two minutes of the
game. The score was tied. The Falcons made
a basket. I cheered. Then the Coyotes made
a basket. The Falcons tried for another
basket. The Coyotes blocked them. The
Falcons could give up. They could try again.
The Falcons really wanted to win so they took
another shot. The Coyotes tried to block it.
The ball dropped into the basket. The Falcons
won in the last five seconds of the game!

_____

_____

_____

_____

_____

_____

_____

_____

Capital Letters

📖 Use Handbook pages 276–277.

- Read the announcement.
- Rewrite the announcement. Use capital letters correctly.

---

1. Join captain Michael s. riley for whale-watching on the <u>Star Cruiser</u>.

2. his crew will answer Any questions about whales.

3. ms. lisa Ramírez

4. mr. Samuel thal

5. Dr. richard zauk

6. what does one passenger say?

7. "it's a great trip."

8. "i can't wait to go again."

9. "next time, i will take my mom and dad."

10. All aboard! we sail at 9 a.m. sharp.

Join Captain Michael S. Riley for whale-watching on the <u>Star Cruiser</u>.

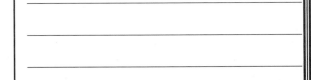

© Hampton-Brown

Capital Letters

📖 Use Handbook page 278.

- **Read the paragraph.**
- **Rewrite the paragraph. Use capital letters correctly.**

If you come to the state of virginia, you'll see a lot of history. Take a boat ride along the chesapeake bay and up the james river. Stop at jamestown, the first permanent English settlement in america. It is part of the colonial national historic park. There you can explore life-size models of three historic ships. Settlers from england sailed here on the susan constant, the godspeed, and the discovery. Take a short drive on the colonial parkway. If you stop at a place called colonial williamsburg, you'll find out how the colonists lived around the time of the American Revolution. So come and visit, and bring your camera!

_____

_____

_____

_____

_____

_____

_____

_____

_____

_____

_____

_____

_____

Name _____ Date _____

Capital Letters

📖 Use Handbook page 279.

■ Look at the chart.

■ Read each address on the left. Rewrite the address on the right. Use abbreviations.

Elena Garcia
218 Sedgewick Pl.
Medford, NJ 08055

Amy Burke
19 Danford St.
Chicago, IL 60625

	Address Without Abbreviations	Address With Abbreviations
1.	Gigi Gallego 302 East San Antonio Drive Seaside, California 93955	Gigi Gallego 302 E. San Antonio Dr. Seaside, CA 93955
2.	Paul Timmins 11479 Rodeo Boulevard San Antonio, Texas 78249	
3.	Joan Matthews 47 South Pelican Street Orlando, Florida 32817	
4.	Frank Miller 98 Washington Square New York, New York 10107	
5.	Andy Ibarra 867 Freedom Lane Boston, Massachusetts 02125	
6.	Brandon Blake 36 West University Avenue Madison, Wisconsin 53706	
7.	Lucas Inouye 44 Kapa Kapa Court Honolulu, Hawaii 96822	
8.	Amanda Rydell 2284 North Covington Place Lincoln, Nebraska 68505	

© Hampton-Brown

Capital Letters

📖 Use Handbook page 280.

- **Read the sentences.**
- **Rewrite the sentences. Use capital letters correctly.**

1. Starting in september, Shawna will be very busy.

   Starting in September, Shawna will be very busy.

2. On labor day, her family is having a picnic.

3. She has a girl scout meeting on the first thursday of the month.

4. The Milltown science club meets the following Friday.

5. Shawna's basketball team, the tigers, plays against the eagles a week later.

6. On sept. 30, she's going with Mom to bill's party supplies and andre's bakery.

7. They'll shop for her brother's birthday party, which will be at his cub scout meeting on saturday.

8. Then it'll be october and all Shawna has to do is get ready for halloween!

Sentence Punctuation

📖 Use Handbook page 282.

- Read each sentence.
- Write the correct punctuation mark at the end of the sentence.

1. I wish I had a way to earn some money__.__

2. Wow, look at this ad in the newspaper___

3. This job looks perfect for you___

4. What does it say___

5. The Community Center is looking for helpers___

6. What do they want the helpers to do___

7. They want help cleaning up the park___

8. How much are they paying___

9. They will pay the helpers $5.25 an hour___

10. When do they want people to work___

11. They can use help on the weekends___

12. That sounds great___

13. You could go down there right now___

14. Maybe some of my friends would like to help, too___

15. Are Ramon, Sylvia, and Judy looking for work___

16. Yes. I'll go call them___

The Period and the Comma

📖 Use Handbook page 283.

- **Read the letter.**
- **Use the proofreading marks to add the missing periods and commas.**

Proofreading Mark	
⋀	Add a comma.
⊙	Add a period.

17 North Avenue

New York ⋀ NY 10033

November 18 2003

Dear Aunt Ruth

    Thank you for the wonderful birthday present! Your check for $20.00 was just what I needed to buy some skates. With the $1500 I earned by walking Mr Davi's dog raking leaves and running errands I can buy the skates. They are on sale for $3500.

    You'd really like the skates. They are black with red wheels blue shoelaces and silver stripes. My friends Tiffany Max Pablo and B J all have skates. I hope we can skate 1000000 miles!

    Thank you again. I can't wait to see you when you visit us again on July 9 2004.

               Love

               Kelly

The Comma

Use Handbook pages 284–285.

- Read what the people are saying.
- Use the proofreading mark to add the missing commas.

Jane   Mr. Storm

This is the Dog Information Hot Line⋏isn't it?

        Yes it is. I'm Mr. Storm.

Mr. Storm my name is Jane. I'm walking a big brown dog named Buster. He's a great dog but he's very hard to handle. My friend Aaron said "Call the Hot Line and they'll help you." You do give people advice don't you?

        Yes, I do. Use a six-foot-long strong leash when you walk the dog and hold it with both hands. As my wife says "Keep the dog close so you can handle him better."

Thanks Mr. Storm. I'll ask his owners if they have the right kind of leash or I'll get one myself.

        Good. Let me know how you're doing won't you?

Oh you bet I will. Thanks again.

The Colon and the Apostrophe

📖 Use Handbook pages 285–286.

■ **Rewrite the letter. Add the missing colons and apostrophes.**

177 North Avenue
New York, NY 10033
December 3, 2004

Ms. Hansons Books
814 Locust Ave.
Corpus Christi, TX 78374

Dear Ms. Hanson

I read your ad in my fathers paper. Id like to order these books
    1. <u>All Bicycle Owners Fix-It Guide</u> by Donna Quinn
    2. <u>How to Organize a Bike Rodeo</u> by the U. S. Bike Club
Call me at (212) 555-3399 after 330 p.m. weekdays to tell me
when youre mailing them.

        Sincerely,

        Aaron Jackson

_____

_____

_____

_____

_____

_____

_____

_____

_____

_____

_____

_____

Underline and Quotation Marks

📖 Use Handbook page 287.

- Read the story.
- Add the missing underlines and quotation marks.

Aaron and his friends read the chapters in Aaron's book, How to Organize a Bike Rodeo. Bobby and Max read "Best Places for a Rodeo." Sam read Advertising the Rodeo. Pablo and Aaron read Games and Prizes. Then they all met to talk about it.

Let's ask Mr. Liu if we can have the rodeo at the school next Saturday, said Aaron. It has a big, safe parking lot.

Okay, said Max. I'll ask The Daily News or Pinewood Gazette to do ads for us.

Maybe the bike shop will give us the prizes. I'll check, said Bobby.

The boys got ready for the rodeo. They made up a song called Ride, Ride, Ride Your Bike. They made up a sign like the one in the book. The sign said, Bicycle Rodeo. Fun for All! They cleaned the school parking lot.

After the rodeo was over, Aaron said, That was a lot of fun.

It was a great idea," said Mr. Liu. I think we should do it every year!"

Alphabetical Order

📖 Use Handbook page 296.

- Look at the words in each box.
- Write the words in alphabetical order.

| Venus |
| Mars |
| Earth |
| Neptune |
| Pluto |

| shuttle |
| star |
| Saturn |
| sun |
| space |

1. *Earth*

2. _____

3. _____

4. _____

5. _____

11. _____

12. _____

13. _____

14. _____

15. _____

| mineral |
| mud |
| meteor |
| matter |
| moisture |

| country |
| comet |
| colony |
| constellation |
| code |

6. _____

7. _____

8. _____

9. _____

10. _____

16. _____

17. _____

18. _____

19. _____

20. _____

© Hampton-Brown

How to Take Notes

📖 Use Handbook pages 298–299.

■ **Read each question.**

■ **Write the answer.**

1. Why should you take notes when you read or research a topic?

   to help you remember the facts and details

2. What should you do to show that you copied the exact words from something you read?

   _____

3. Look at the notecards on page 299. What is the research question?

   _____

4. What comes after the research question?

   _____

5. Why should you write down the title, author, and page number of a book?

   _____

6. Who wrote the book *Mars*?

   _____

7. Where on the notecards should you write the details and facts you find?

   _____

8. What is one fact from the book *Mars*?

   _____

9. Where can you find the article "Next Stop: Mars"?

   _____

10. Which fact shows exact words copied from a source? Write the fact.

    _____

© Hampton-Brown

How to Take Notes

📖 Use Handbook pages 298–299.

- Read the article on Handbook page 327.

- Use the notecards to take notes.

What is Mars?
"Mars," *The World Book Encyclopedia*, Vol. 13,
   page 223
   —

   —

   —

How big is Mars?

   —

   —

   —

Making an Outline

📖 Use Handbook pages 300–301.

■ Read the Main Ideas, Details, and Related Details in the chart.

■ Finish the outline for a research report about the first moon landing.

Main Ideas	Details	Related Details
What the astronauts did First humans land on moon	July 20, 1969 American astronauts Took pictures Lunar module called Eagle Left American flag in ground	Neil Armstrong Edwin Aldrin Rocks Soil

A Trip to the Moon

I. _____

    A. _American astronauts_____

        1. _____

        2. _____

    B. _____

    C. _____

II. _____

    A. _Collected samples_____

        1. _____

        2. _____

    B. _____

    C. _____

Making an Outline

📖 Use Handbook pages 300–301.

■ **Read the notes on the notecards.**

■ **Use the notes to make an outline.**

On the Moon

I. <u>The moon's surface</u>

    A. _____

        1. _____

        _____

        2. _____

        _____

    B. _____

        1. _____

        _____

        2. _____

II. _____

    A. _____

    _____

    B. _____

        1. _____

        2. _____

What is the moon's surface like?
Visual Encyclopedia of Science, page 176
— closest side to Earth has large areas of lava
— farthest side has huge craters and mountains

What is the moon's surface like?
World Book Encyclopedia, Vol. 13, page 784
— near side has flat plains and rocky soil
— far side called the <u>highlands</u>, it's mountainous

Does the moon have an atmosphere?
Visual Encyclopedia of Science, page 177
— no atmosphere
— without wind or weather, astronauts' footprints last a long time

Does the moon have an atmosphere?
World Book Encyclopedia, Vol. 13, page 788
— little or no atmosphere
— no weather, clouds, rain, or wind
— no air to carry sound, astronauts use radios

Card Catalog

📖 Use Handbook pages 306–307.

- Read each question.
- Write the answer.

1. How can you find out if the library has a book you want?

   Look for a card about the book
   in the card catalog.

2. Does the copyright date give the year a book was published or the number of pages in a book?

   _____

3. What number tells you what section of the library a book is in?

   _____

4. How do you know if a book is in the children's section?

   _____

5. What does **KIT** stand for in the call number for Satoshi Kitamura's book?

   _____

6. How are fiction books arranged on the library shelves?

   _____

7. How do you know if a book is in the nonfiction section of the library?

   _____

8. Would you find the book *Are We Moving to Mars?* in the library shelves with other books about the subject "Technology" or "Literature"?

   _____

Card Catalog

Use Handbook page 308.

- Look at the cards from a card catalog.
- Answer the questions.

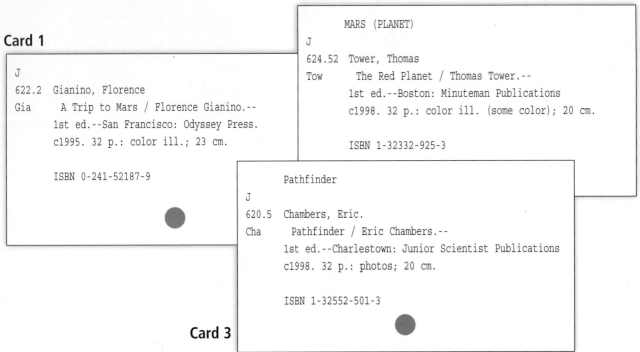

Card 1

```
J
622.2  Gianino, Florence
Gia      A Trip to Mars / Florence Gianino.--
        1st ed.--San Francisco: Odyssey Press.
        c1995. 32 p.: color ill.; 23 cm.

        ISBN 0-241-52187-9
```

Card 2

```
         MARS (PLANET)
J
624.52  Tower, Thomas
Tow       The Red Planet / Thomas Tower.--
         1st ed.--Boston: Minuteman Publications
         c1998. 32 p.: color ill. (some color); 20 cm.

         ISBN 1-32332-925-3
```

```
         Pathfinder
J
620.5   Chambers, Eric.
Cha       Pathfinder / Eric Chambers.--
         1st ed.--Charlestown: Junior Scientist Publications
         c1998. 32 p.: photos; 20 cm.

         ISBN 1-32552-501-3
```

Card 3

1. Is **Card 1** an author card or a title card? *author card*

2. Is **Card 2** a subject card or an author card? _____

3. How do you know that the book on **Card 2** is nonfiction? _____

   _____

4. What kind of card is **Card 3**? _____

5. Who wrote the book on **Card 2**? _____

6. What book did Florence Gianino write? _____

7. Would a subject card for PLUTO come before or after the card for MARS? _____

8. Would a card for a book by Mary Borgia come before or after the card

   for the book by Florence Gianino? _____

Parts of a Book: Title Page and Table of Contents

📖 Use Handbook pages 312–313.

Look at Handbook pages 312–313.
Then follow the directions for each part below.

■ **Find the title page in the front of your Handbook.**

■ **Finish the sentences.**

1. The title of the book is _____ .

2. The publisher is _____ .

■ **Look at the table of contents on Handbook pages 4–11.**

■ **Finish the sentences.**

3. Chapter 1 is mostly about _____ .

4. Chapter 2 begins on _____ .

5. In Chapter 2, the kinds of graphs you can read about are _____

_____ .

6. Three kinds of writing you can find out about in Chapter 3 are _____

_____ .

7. Chapter 5 is all about _____ .

8. The chapter that tells about finding information on the Internet

is _____ .

9. The section that begins on page 290 is called _____ .

10. The Index begins on _____ .

Parts of a Book: Index

📖 Use Handbook page 314.

- Read about an index on Handbook page 314.
- Turn to Handbook pages 405–413.
- Answer the questions.

1. How are subjects listed in an index?

in alphabetical order _____

2. Does the subject "Book review" come before or after

the subject "Biography"? _____

3. What are the related details listed for the subject "Letters (to people)"?

_____

_____

4. On which pages can you find information about business letters?

_____

5. Find the pages about business letters. Name the parts of a business letter.

_____

_____

6. Find "World Wide Web" in the index. What other subject does it say to look up?

_____

7. On which pages can you find information about the subject "Internet"?

_____

8. Look up the pages about the "Internet." Which page tells you what

the World Wide Web is? What is the World Wide Web?

_____

_____

Parts of a Book: Glossary

📖 Use Handbook page 315.

- ■ **Work with a partner.**

- ■ **Write the words in the box in alphabetical order. Then look up each kind of writing in Chapter 3 of the Handbook.**

- ■ **Write a definition for each entry to make a glossary.**

Kinds of Writing	
Fairy Tale	Autobiography
Play	Tall Tale
Personal Narrative	Fantasy
Folk Tale	Biography

GLOSSARY

1. Autobiography — the true story of your own life, written by you.

2. _____

3. _____

4. _____

5. _____

6. _____

7. _____

8. _____

© Hampton-Brown

Almanac

📖 Use Handbook pages 316–317.

- **What is an almanac like?
  How can you use it?**

- **Finish the sentences to tell about
  an almanac.**

1. An almanac is a _____*book of facts*_____ .

2. It has information about many different

   _____ .

3. An almanac has up-to-date information because it is rewritten

   _____ .

4. To find out if an almanac has information about a subject, first look up

   key words in the _____ .

5. Then turn to _____ for the article in the book.

6. Next, _____ the article to see if it has the

   information you want.

7. Use the _____ and the _____

   in the article to find the main ideas.

8. Look for _____ and _____

   to help explain information.

9. Also look for _____ and _____

   that might have useful information.

10. If the article is useful for your report, _____

    and _____ .

Almanac

📖 Use Handbook pages 316–317.

- **Read the questions.**
- **Use the almanac pages in your Handbook to answer the questions.**

1. How can you find the article in the almanac?

look up the key words in the index _____

2. What is the title of the article? _____

3. What does the diagram on the first page of the article show?

_____

4. Is Earth or Mars farther from the sun? _____

5. Under which heading can you find out about the sun?

_____

6. What is the diameter of the sun? _____

7. What are three types of facts listed for each planet on the second page?

_____

8. How long does it take for Earth to revolve around the sun?

_____

9. Look at the special features. What is one interesting fact you learned?

_____

10. Would you read these pages carefully if you were researching facts about the Earth? Why or why not?

_____

_____

Atlas: Physical and Political Maps

📖 Use Handbook pages 318–319.

■ Read the questions.

■ Use the maps in your Handbook to answer the questions.

1. What does a physical map show?

the rivers, forests, mountains, lowlands, coastlines, or oceans of a place

2. What does a map scale show?

_____

3. What are the names of the landforms shown on the physical map?

_____

_____

4. What does a political map show?

_____

5. What is the first step in finding a place on a political map?

_____

6. What special code would you use to find the city of Brunswick

on the map? _____

7. Will the letter in a special code like **J-5** be between two lines of latitude

or between two lines of longitude?

_____

8. Do the lines of longitude on a political map go from east to west

or from north to south? _____

Dictionary

📖 Use Handbook pages 322–323.

- **Read the questions.**
- **Use the dictionary pages in your Handbook to answer the questions.**

1. What is a dictionary?

a book filled with information about words

2. How are the words in a dictionary organized?

_____

3. Would you find the word *gravity* in the front, middle, or back part

of a dictionary? _____

4. In which part of a dictionary would you find the word *orbit*?

_____

5. What do the guide words on each dictionary page tell you?

_____

6. Look at the guide words on page 322. Which word comes last

on the dictionary page? _____

7. Does the entry for *spacewalk* come before or after *spacecraft*? _____

8. Look at the guide words on page 323. Why is the word *spamming*

on this page?

_____

9. Which two entry words is the word *spamming* between?

_____

10. Would the guide words on the page that comes <u>after</u> the one on page 323

be **sourball** • **South Pole** or **Spanish** • **speak**? _____

Dictionary

📖 Use Handbook pages 324–325.

- Look at the dictionary pages in your Handbook. Find the entry for each word.
- Follow the directions.

space

1. Write the definition for meaning 2.

_____

2. Write a sentence using meaning 4.

_____

_____

3. Tell the word's part of speech. _____

4. Write the plural form of the word used as a noun. _____

5. Show how to pronounce the singular form of the word. _____

spacesuit

6. Write the definition.

_____

_____

7. Write a sentence using the meaning.

_____

_____

8. Tell the word's part of speech. _____

9. Write the plural form of the word. _____

10. Show how to pronounce the singular form of the word. _____

Encyclopedia

📖 Use Handbook pages 326–327.

- Read each question.
- Mark the answer.

1. What is each book in an encyclopedia called?
- ⬤ volume
- ◯ article
- ◯ topic

2. What does each volume in an encyclopedia contain?
- ◯ stories
- ◯ articles
- ◯ questions

3. What is the last volume in a set of encyclopedias called?
- ◯ index
- ◯ dictionary
- ◯ almanac

4. In which order would these articles appear in volume 1?
- ◯ asteroid, atom, aircraft
- ◯ aircraft, asteroid, atom
- ◯ aircraft, atom, asteroid

5. Which volume would have an article about Mars?
- ◯ volume 1
- ◯ volume 13
- ◯ volume 21

6. What are the words at the top of each page called?
- ◯ guide words
- ◯ headings
- ◯ entry words

7. What is the title of an article called?
- ◯ a guide word
- ◯ the heading
- ◯ an entry word

8. What is the title of each section of an article called?
- ◯ a guide word
- ◯ the heading
- ◯ an entry word

9. What is the entry word for the article on **Handbook** page 327?
- ◯ Mars
- ◯ Mars at a glance
- ◯ orbit and rotation

10. What is the article on **Handbook** page 327 mostly about?
- ◯ space missions
- ◯ size, orbit, and location of Mars
- ◯ the solar system

Telephone Directory

📖 **Use Handbook pages 330–331.**

- Pretend that you are planning a party.

- Write a list of the businesses you would call and their phone numbers. Write the list in alphabetical order.

PAPADATOS—PATRICK

Papadatos Demetrios	622-8252
Papa Joe's Party Supplies	622-1898
Pappas Lambros	622-8400
Pardo Jeanna	622-2623
Paredes Ignacio	622-7751
Park Jin Ki	622-0003
Parkway Little League	622-8002
Parna M	622-8989
Party Central	622-5545
PARTY TIME	
111 Centre St	622-0189
Party Works	622-4587

Party—Patio 567

Party Supplies—Retail and Rental

AA Rentals
"Everything You Need"
Tables • Chairs • China • Linen • Games • Decorations
125 Greenwood 622-8909

Balloons for You 622-9475

Party Time
Party Supplies • Tents
111 Centre St 622-0189

AA Rentals, 622-8909

_____

_____

_____

_____

- Is there anything else you need for your party? Write some other guide words you would use to look up businesses in the yellow pages.

_____ _____

_____ _____

Drafting

📖 Use Handbook page 97.

- **Tell how to make a mask.**

- **Write the directions. Be sure to include the materials you need and to put the steps in order.**

What kind of mask is it?

_____

What materials do you need to make the mask?

_____   _____

_____   _____

_____   _____

_____

What are the steps for making the mask?
What should someone do to make it?

1. _____

_____

2. _____

_____

3. _____

_____

4. _____

_____

5. _____

_____

Revising

📖 Use Handbook pages 100–102.

Revise these directions. Be sure the steps are clear and are in the correct order.

Revising Marks	
∧	Add.
⌒	Move to here.
⌐	Replace with this.
ꜱ	Take out.
⊙	Add a period.

How to Make a Headband

You'll need: paper   stickers   glue   ruler
glitter   string

3 inches

Cut a strip of paper the same length as the string.

First, use the string to measure your head. Make the strip

inches wide. Decorate the strip with stickers. Fourth, the ends

of the strip together. The glue dries. Put on your headband.

Editing and Proofreading

📖 Use Handbook page 106.

Proofread these directions. Be sure to use commands and add any missing commas.

Proofreading Marks			
∧	Add.	○	Check spelling.
⋏	Add a comma.	/	Make lowercase.
⊙	Add a period.	¶	Start a new paragraph.
≡	Capitalize.	ꜱ	Take out.

How to Make a Halloween Mask

You'll need: paper plate   paper scraps   scissors   string
yarn   glue   markers

1. The paper plate goes up to your face. Have someone

   mark your eyes nose and mouth.

2. Put the plate down Then the holes.

Decorate the plate with paper scraps markers or yarn.

4. poke a hole on each side and attach the strng.

5. The mask is for halloween.

© Hampton-Brown

Name _____ Date _____

Drafting

📖 Use Handbook page 97.

- Write about the first time you did something.

- Use lots of details to tell when it happened, what it was like, and how you felt.

The first time I _____

was _____

_____ .

It was _____

_____ .

↓

At first, when I _____

_____

_____ .

Then, _____

_____ .

↓

Finally, _____

_____

_____ .

I felt _____

_____ .

Revising

📖 Use Handbook pages 100–102.

Revise this personal narrative. Be sure to add details to give a good picture of what happened.

Revising Marks	
∧	Add.
⟳	Move to here.
⤬	Replace with this.
⤸	Take out.
⊙	Add a period.

On my birthday, I went bowling for the first time.

I had to use both hands to pick up that ball!

Then I tried to roll the ball down the alley.

The third time, I did it! The first time, I dropped

the ball behind. The second time, it went into

the gutter! The ball rolled in a line toward the pins.

Finally, I knocked pins down! Now I like to bowl!

Editing and Proofreading

📖 Use Handbook page 106.

Proofread this personal narrative. Be sure to use pronouns correctly.

Proofreading Marks			
∧	Add.	◯	Check spelling.
⩘	Add a comma.	/	Make lowercase.
⊙	Add a period.	¶	Start a new paragraph.
≡	Capitalize.	⤸	Take out.

Last year, I won the school Spelling Bee. They was not easy

to win mrs. Lee gave we hard words to spell, like *receive* and

occasion. He is our principal Mom had helped I practice, so i spelled

all the words correctly. i was really proud of yourself.

© Hampton-Brown

Drafting

📖 Use Handbook page 97.

- **What news do you want to share with someone you know? What do you want to ask the person?**

- **Write a friendly letter.**

_____

_____

_____ , _____

Dear _____ ,

    I've got news for you! _____

_____

_____

_____

    How are you? _____

_____

_____

_____

_____

_____

_____

© Hampton-Brown

Revising

📖 Use Handbook pages 100–102.

Revise this part of a friendly letter. Be sure to use questions so Elinor will write back.

Revising Marks	
∧	Add.
᧖	Move to here.
⌄	Replace with this.
ꜱ	Take out.
⊙	Add a period.

Elinor,

We're coming to New York City in the May. I don't no what

to pack. It might be warm or cool in May. I can't wait to see you!

Sami

Editing and Proofreading

📖 Use Handbook page 106.

Proofread this friendly letter. Be sure to use capital letters and punctuation correctly.

Proofreading Marks			
∧	Add.	◯	Check spelling.
⋀	Add a comma.	∕	Make lowercase.
⊙	Add a period.	¶	Start a new paragraph.
≡	Capitalize.	ꜱ	Take out.

2435 oak Street

San Jose, ca 95110

january 10 2004

Dear Keiko

My family is getting ready for Kwanzaa. That's when we

celebrate our african ancestry and spend lots of time together.

What's your favorite holiday in japan

Your friend

Yolanda

Drafting

📖 Use Handbook page 97.

- **What is important to you? What do you want changed? What should someone do to change it?**

- **Write a persuasive paragraph.**

1. Tell your opinion or how you feel about something.

I think that the _____

should _____

_____

_____ .

2. Give reasons for your opinion. Tell why you want something changed.

It is important to _____

because _____

_____

_____

_____

_____

_____

_____ .

3. Tell what you want someone to do.

Please _____

_____

_____

_____ .

Revising

📖 Use Handbook pages 100–102.

Revise this persuasive paragraph. Be sure to add persuasive words and reasons for the opinion.

Revising Marks	
∧	Add.
⌆	Move to here.
⌒	Replace with this.
⤸	Take out.
⊙	Add a period.

We can only check out two books at a time. I think that the library rule for checking out books is unfair. This is a problem because we have to keep coming back to get more. Also, we like to find lots of facts for our research reports. Here's another reason. Reading more books helps students. We would like to change this rule. Ask the librarian to let us check out more books at a time!

Editing and Proofreading

📖 Use Handbook page 106.

Proofread this persuasive paragraph. Be sure to add helping verbs where they are needed.

Proofreading Marks			
∧	Add.	⬭	Check spelling.
⋏	Add a comma.	∕	Make lowercase.
⊙	Add a period.	¶	Start a new paragraph.
≡	Capitalize.	⤸	Take out.

Our school not have enough computers Right now, there are only five computers, and everyone waits in line to use them. Every student have a chance to use a computter when he or she needs to. If we had more computers, all of us do our best work. we finish our reports on time, too!

Drafting

📖 **Use Handbook page 97.**

■ **Draw a picture of your favorite place, animal, season, or food.**

■ **Write a poem to tell what it is like.**

┌───┐
│   │
│   │
│   │
│   │
│   │
│   │
│   │
│   │
│   │
│   │
└───┘

_____
(title)

1. _____
(topic)

2. _____
(words that tell what the topic is like)

3. _____
(more words that tell what the topic is like)

4. _____
(more words that tell what the topic is like)

5. _____
(topic)

Revising

📖 Use Handbook pages 100–102.

Revise this poem. Be sure the details give a good picture of the topic.

Revising Marks	
∧	Add.
⌕	Move to here.
⌐	Replace with this.
⤶	Take out.
⊙	Add a period.

City Senses

See the buildings and the bridges.

Smell the food coming from the restaurant.

Listen to the cars passing along on the street.

This is where I live.

Editing and Proofreading

📖 Use Handbook page 106.

Proofread this poem. Be sure to spell plural nouns correctly.

Proofreading Marks			
∧	Add.	⟲	Check spelling.
∧	Add a comma.	/	Make lowercase.
⊙	Add a period.	¶	Start a new paragraph.
≡	Capitalize.	⤶	Take out.

Two Pizzas

pizzas   Pizzas

Eight slice each   Order them now

Two kind of melted cheese   The child are hungry

Peppers, olives, no anchovys   They'll them right from the boxs

Pizza   Pizzas

Drafting

📖 Use Handbook page 97.

- **Make up some characters and a setting that are like people and places you know.**

- **Write a story. Tell about events that could happen in real life.**

1. Name the characters. Tell about the place and time.

_____ and _____

were at the _____

_____ .

It was _____

_____ .

2. Tell what the problem is.

_____ , but _____

_____

_____

_____ .

3. Tell what happens. What do the characters say and do?

_____

_____

_____

_____

_____

_____

_____

4. Tell what finally happens. Tell how the problem is solved.

_____

so _____

_____ .

Revising

📖 Use Handbook pages 100–102.

Revise this story. Be sure the details and dialogue seem like real life.

Revising Marks	
∧	Add.
�⟩	Move to here.
⌐	Replace with this.
⤵	Take out.
⊙	Add a period.

Grandma said good morning to Ryan. She wanted to know why he was frowning. "What's wrong?"

"I'm nervous about the volleyball game," Ryan said. "When it's my turn to serve, I can't do it."

"I was a volleyball champ when I was younger," Grandma said. She told Ryan that she could help him practice.

Editing and Proofreading

📖 Use Handbook page 106.

Proofread this story. Be sure to use quotation marks and contractions correctly.

Proofreading Marks			
∧	Add.	◯	Check spelling.
⋏	Add a comma.	/	Make lowercase.
⊙	Add a period.	¶	Start a new paragraph.
≡	Capitalize.	⤵	Take out.

Carlo Mendicino wasn't looking forward to summer vacation.

I don't want school to be over, he told his mom. "Im really going to miss my art class. When carlo got home from school, his mom said "I have a big surprise. Ive enrolled you in art school this Summer.

"Thats great, Mom. Thanks. Now it'll be a great summer."

Drafting

📖 Use Handbook page 97.

- ■ Write about something that happened to you on a special day.

- ■ Use lots of details to tell when something happened, what things were like, and how you felt.

On _____ , _____

_____

_____

_____

_____

↓

Then, _____

_____

_____

_____

_____

↓

Finally, _____

_____

_____

_____

_____

Revising

📖 Use Handbook pages 100–102.

Revise this personal narrative. Be sure the details give a good picture of what happened.

Revising Marks	
∧	Add.
ᴐ	Move to here.
⌐	Replace with this.
✎	Take out.
⊙	Add a period.

On Thanksgiving Day, my family went to my aunt's house who is my mom's sister. I could smell the food, but we had to wait to eat. My stomach was making noises. Then, it was time to eat. I piled mashed potatoes, turkey, gravy, cranberries, and stuffing on my plate. It tasted good. Finally, I took a bite.

Editing and Proofreading

📖 Use Handbook page 106.

Proofread this personal narrative. Be sure to use pronouns correctly.

Proofreading Marks			
∧	Add.	◯	Check spelling.
⁁	Add a comma.	/	Make lowercase.
⊙	Add a period.	¶	Start a new paragraph.
≡	Capitalize.	✎	Take out.

Dad bought a piñata. She bought it for my birthday party. The piñata looked like a swan. It's beak was orange and its feathers were white My friend and me took turns hitting the piñata while my Dad pulled it up and down. Then when i hit the piñata, they broke open. Finally, us got lots of candy!

© Hampton-Brown

Drafting

📖 Use Handbook page 97.

- Write about your classmate.

- Use lots of details to tell what that person looks like and likes to do. Tell how that person is special.

Guess Who?

This person has _____ eyes and _____ hair

and is _____.

I like the way my classmate _____

_____

and _____

_____.

This person loves to _____

_____.

My classmate is also very good at _____

_____.

I know this because _____

_____.

The most surprising thing about this person is _____

_____

_____

_____.

Can you guess who this person is?

Revising

📖 Use Handbook pages 100–102.

- Look at the boy on Handbook pages 20–21.
- Then revise this character sketch. Be sure the details and examples give a good picture of what the boy is like.

Revising Marks	
∧	Add.
↶	Move to here.
↖	Replace with this.
ꜱ	Take out.
⊙	Add a period.

The boy is about five feet tall and has blond hair and eyes.

He really likes sports and is a good player.

This boy loves to write. He often writes down stories his family

tells. He has a lot of relatives. Sometimes at school he stays inside

so he can write stories.

Editing and Proofreading

📖 Use Handbook page 106.

Proofread this paragraph. Be sure each subject agrees with its verb.

Proofreading Marks			
∧	Add.	⬡	Check spelling.
⅄	Add a comma.	/	Make lowercase.
⊙	Add a period.	¶	Start a new paragraph.
≡	Capitalize.	ꜱ	Take out.

My friend has emerald green eyes and a beautiful smile

She are a very happy person. she is also the friendlyest person

I knows.

She like to play with her dog Sundae. He have a White belly,

Yellow sides, and a Brown back. My friend's brothers thinks that

the dog looks like an ice cream sundae!

Drafting

📖 Use Handbook page 97.

- **Write a tall tale.**
- **Use lots of details to make your character and the events unbelievable!**

1. Draw a picture of your tall tale character.

[drawing box]

2. Tell what your character wants.

_____ wants to

_____ because _____

_____ .

3. Tell what the character does to get what he or she wants.

So one day _____

_____

_____ .

Next, _____

_____ .

Then, _____

_____

_____ .

4. Tell what happens in the end. Does your character get what he or she wants?

Finally, _____

_____

_____ .

Revising

📖 Use Handbook pages 100–102.

Revise this tall tale. Be sure to use synonyms to make the story entertaining and impossible to believe.

Revising Marks	
∧	Add.
↶	Move to here.
⌐	Replace with this.
⤴	Take out.
⊙	Add a period.

Tiny Jack was little, but he was strong. Once he went into an

ant hole in Kentucky. No one saw him for three days. He said that

he had built a children's playground. When he finally came home.

When the children went into the hole, they found a big cave! It was

the cave, Mammoth-Flint Ridge Cave, which is over 190 miles long!

Editing and Proofreading

📖 Use Handbook page 106.

Proofread this tall tale. Look for short sentences that can be combined with a comma and *and*, *but*, or *or*.

Proofreading Marks			
∧	Add.	◯	Check spelling.
⩜	Add a comma.	/	Make lowercase.
⊙	Add a period.	¶	Start a new paragraph.
≡	Capitalize.	⤴	Take out.

Go to Arizona. You'll see the Painted Desert. Why is it called

that Well, Fine Fran loved the desert. She hated all the yellow dirt.

She could leave Arizona. She could change the desert's color. Then

she had an idea. Fran pulled a rainbow down from the sky. Then

she swept it across the land. She painted the dessert with all the

colors of the rainbow

© Hampton-Brown

Drafting

📖 Use Handbook page 97.

■ **Write a business letter. Ask someone for the things you need to do your class project.**

_____

_____

_____
(your address and the date)

_____

_____

_____
(address of the business or company)

Dear _____ :

I am a student at _____

_____ . Our class is doing a project to improve our school.

We want to _____

_____ .

Can you donate _____

or _____ ?

Thank you very much for your help.

Sincerely yours,

_____
(your signature)

_____
(your name printed)

Revising

📖 Use Handbook pages 100–102.

Revise the body of this business letter. Be sure to use formal language and make the request clear.

Revising Marks	
∧	Add.
⤸	Move to here.
⤝	Replace with this.
⤳	Take out.
⊙	Add a period.

Our class wants to beautify River School. We are gonna start

planting some flowers and stuff like that in front of the school.

I want you to send us something. We'll also need some tools.

Thanks.

Editing and Proofreading

📖 Use Handbook page 106.

Proofread this business letter. Use capital letters and punctuation correctly.

Proofreading Marks			
∧	Add.	⬭	Check spelling.
∧	Add a comma.	/	Make lowercase.
⊙	Add a period.	¶	Start a new paragraph.
≡	Capitalize.	⤳	Take out.

492 Washington ave.

Chicago IL 60001

september 3, 2003

Zeke's Hardware

562 w. miller St.

Chicago, il 60001

Dear sir or Madam

Our class is cleaning up the trash around Parkview School. Can

Zeke's hardware donate some trash bags We appreciate your help,

Sincerely yours

Kathy Alcantara

Kathy Alcantara

© Hampton-Brown

Drafting

📖 Use Handbook page 97.

- ■ **Write an advertisement for the Class Newspaper.**
- ■ **Follow the steps below.**

Muffins for Sale

Huge, yummy, fresh chocolate chip and blueberry muffins. $1.00 each.

Order from Jessica in Ms. Fernandez's room (Rm. 9). Next day delivery.

1. Draw a picture of what you want to buy, sell, or trade.

2. Name the item. Tell what it is like. Tell how much it costs.

_____

_____

_____

_____

3. Tell what people should do to find out about the item.

_____

_____

_____

_____

Revising

📖 Use Handbook pages 100–102.

Revise this editorial. Be sure to add important details and facts.

Revising Marks	
∧	Add.
∽	Move to here.
⌐	Replace with this.
ꜱ	Take out.
⊙	Add a period.

Fifth Grade Needs Playground Equipment

We think that kids at Jefferson Elementary School need new equipment. Most of the balls are gone. The jump ropes are old. We like to play baseball, but we need things. Please talk to anyone you can. Ask them to help us get what we want.

Editing and Proofreading

📖 Use Handbook page 106.

Proofread this news story. Be sure to use nouns correctly.

Proofreading Marks			
∧	Add.	⟠	Check spelling.
⋏	Add a comma.	/	Make lowercase.
⊙	Add a period.	¶	Start a new paragraph.
≡	Capitalize.	ꜱ	Take out.

Finley project Helps Neighbors

LAREDO, Texas—cata Ortiz was just one of the child from finley Elementary School who participated in Make-a-Difference Day. On october 25, several volunteers and laredo Rotary member gave clothing to 35 familys who were victims of the recent floods. "We were happy to help," said 11-year-old ortiz. "We hope that we can get more person involved next Year."

© Hampton-Brown

Drafting

📖 Use Handbook page 97.

■ **Look at your outline. Use the title, main ideas, and details to write a report.**

Title: _____

Interesting
Introduction: _____

_____

_____

_____

Topic Sentence
for Main Idea I: _____

_____

Detail Sentences: _____

_____

_____

_____

Topic Sentence
for Main Idea II: _____

_____

Detail Sentences: _____

_____

_____

_____

Conclusion That
Tells Each Main
Idea: _____

_____

_____

_____

Name _____ Date _____

Revising

📖 Use Handbook pages 100–102.

Revise these paragraphs from a report. Be sure each paragraph has a topic sentence.

Revising Marks	
∧	Add.
⌂	Move to here.
⌐	Replace with this.
⌡	Take out.
⊙	Add a period.

I. Life on Saturn and Jupiter
   A. Probably none on Saturn
   B. Maybe tiny organisms on Jupiter
II. Rings around Saturn and Jupiter different
   A. Saturn has 7 big rings made of ice
   B. Jupiter has 1 thin ring made of rock

Some scientists don't believe that there are plants or animals on Saturn. However, it's possible that organisms do exist on Jupiter.

Saturn has rings than Jupiter. Both Saturn and Jupiter have rings, but the rings are different. It has seven big rings made of ice. Neptune has rings. Jupiter has only won thin ring made of rock.

Editing and Proofreading

📖 Use Handbook page 106.

Proofread this paragraph. Be sure the correct adjectives are used to compare things.

Proofreading Marks			
∧	Add.	○	Check spelling.
∧	Add a comma.	/	Make lowercase.
⊙	Add a period.	¶	Start a new paragraph.
≡	Capitalize.	⌡	Take out.

The Big Dipper and Little Dipper are groups of stars that look like ladles. Each group has seven stars, but the Big Dipper is bright than the Little Dipper. It's also big. however, the Little Dipper is most important for showing which way is north The more visible star in that group is the North Star, which is almost over the North Pole?

© Hampton-Brown

Name _____ Date _____

Drafting

📖 Use Handbook page 97.

- Look at your diagram. Use it to help you think about what your place is like.

- Write a description of the place. Be sure to use direction words like *right, left, next to, close to, above,* or *below* to tell where things are.

_____
(name of place)

The _____ in _____

is _____ .

When you go there, the first thing you'll see _____

_____

_____ .

If you look _____ you'll see _____

_____

_____

_____ to that you'll see _____

_____

_____ .

Finally, look _____ and you'll see

_____

_____

_____ .

Revising

📖 Use Handbook pages 100–102.

Revise this description. Use lots of details to help the readers imagine that they are there!

Revising Marks	
∧	Add.
⤻	Move to here.
⋀	Replace with this.
⤴	Take out.
⊙	Add a period.

I like to sit on a bench in the park.

There are two trees filled with birds.

There's a pond where some ducks splash and

play. I sit there so the ducks won't notice

me. In the summer sun, the water sparkles.

Editing and Proofreading

📖 Use Handbook page 106.

Proofread this description. Use the correct adjectives to make comparisons. Use the correct prepositions.

Proofreading Marks			
∧	Add.	⬭	Check spelling.
⋏	Add a comma.	/	Make lowercase.
⊙	Add a period.	¶	Start a new paragraph.
≡	Capitalize.	⤴	Take out.

There are four theaters in town, but the Galaxy is the

nicer. It's old than the City cinema. After you walk inside

its glass doors, you'll see the colorful carpet anywhere As

you look beside the lobby, you'll see huge posters near

famous movy stars. Don't forget to look up to see the more

beautiful crystal chandeliers hanging the ceiling.

© Hampton-Brown

Drafting

📖 Use Handbook page 97.

- **What did you discover about something at school? Write a useful tip for a new student that tells what you learned.**

- **Then write a personal narrative to tell how you made the discovery. Use details that tell when, where, and what happened.**

TIP: _____

_____

This is how I found out:

Last _____,

I was _____

when _____

_____.

First I _____

_____.

Then I _____

_____.

That's when I learned that _____

_____

_____

_____.

Revising

📖 Use Handbook pages 100–102.

Revise this personal narrative. Be sure the details give a good picture of what happened.

Revising Marks	
∧	Add.
↶	Move to here.
↖	Replace with this.
⤳	Take out.
⊙	Add a period.

TIP: Ask Mrs. Mitchell to help you find something good to read!

I hated going to the school library. I sat and waited until it was

time to leave. Then I asked Mrs. Mitchell, the lady who worked

there, if there were any books about my favorite animal. I like

horses. She showed me books about ponies, stallions, and pintos.

I never feel bad at the library now.

Editing and Proofreading

📖 Use Handbook page 106.

Proofread this personal narrative. Be sure to use pronouns correctly.

Proofreading Marks			
∧	Add.	⬭	Check spelling.
⊼	Add a comma.	/	Make lowercase.
⊙	Add a period.	¶	Start a new paragraph.
≡	Capitalize.	⤳	Take out.

TIP: Try after-school basketball!

I used to walk home right after school with my sister, Maya.

Her and I didn't know there were things to do after school. Then

one day i heard some kids talk about playing Basketball after school.

so that day, we stayed to see for themselves The kids asked us to

play with they! Maya and me didn't know how to play basketball but

our new friends taught we.

© Hampton-Brown

Drafting

📖 Use Handbook page 97.

■ **Look at your KWLQ chart.**

■ **Use the details and facts to write sentences and paragraphs for a biography.**

Our Guest: _____

1. Name the person. Tell when and where he or she was born.

_____

_____

_____

2. Tell how the person learned his or her job.

_____

_____

_____

_____

_____

_____

3. Tell what the person does now or what his or her job is like.

_____

_____

_____

_____

_____

_____

Revising

📖 Use Handbook pages 100–102.

Revise this biography. Use the chart to check the facts. Be sure to add sequence words.

Revising Marks	
∧	Add.
↰	Move to here.
↖	Replace with this.
↵	Take out.
⊙	Add a period.

l
What I Learned

• Born in Italy, 1952.
• Went to New York at 18.
• Was a waiter, then a cook.
• Bought a restaurant at 30. Named it "Nana's Kitchen."

When he was 18 he moved to New York. Roy Giacone was born in Spain in 1952. He worked in a small restaurant in the city as a waiter. He became a cook. He bought his own restaurant when he was 20. Roy named it "The Kitchen" after his grandmother.

Editing and Proofreading

📖 Use Handbook page 106.

Proofread this biography. Be sure the verbs are in the correct tense.

Proofreading Marks			
∧	Add.	⬭	Check spelling.
⩘	Add a comma.	/	Make lowercase.
⊙	Add a period.	¶	Start a new paragraph.
≡	Capitalize.	↵	Take out.

Tamara Lewis is born in 1958 in California. As a young girl, Tamara loves to study plants, buggs, and animals. After high school, Tamara goes to the University of washington to study biology. After she graduated, Tamara becomes a biologist For a company called Bio Gene

Drafting

📖 Use Handbook page 97.

■ **What do you want changed? Write a business letter to tell how you feel about it and what you want someone to do.**

_____

_____

_____

(your address and the date)

_____

_____

(address of the business or group)

Dear Sir or Madam:

 I think that _____

_____ .

 I think this way because _____

_____ .

Also, _____

_____

_____ .

 Please _____

_____

_____ .

Sincerely,

_____

(your signature)

_____

(your name printed)

Revising

📖 Use Handbook pages 100–102.

Revise this paragraph from a persuasive business letter. Be sure to use persuasive words.

Revising Marks	
∧	Add.
⌒	Move to here.
⌐	Replace with this.
ꜱ	Take out.
⊙	Add a period.

I think the school needs to buy some computers for our class.

It's good for us to learn how to use them! We want computers so we

can do research and write reports. Order some computers for us.

Editing and Proofreading

📖 Use Handbook page 106.

Proofread this letter. Use capital letters and punctuation correctly.

Proofreading Marks			
∧	Add.	◯	Check spelling.
⋏	Add a comma.	╱	Make lowercase.
⊙	Add a period.	¶	Start a new paragraph.
≡	Capitalize.	ꜱ	Take out.

4937 Rancho st.

Barstow, CA 98773

April 27 2004

City Council

22001 S. Sunset St.

Barstow, Ca 98773

dear Mrs. Ruiz,

I feel that we need a new city park. now kids are playing in

the street. That's very dangerous Please tell the city Council that

we must have a safe place to play.

With best regards

Nicholas Benton

Nicholas Benton

© Hampton-Brown

Drafting

📖 Use Handbook page 97.

■ Look at your story map.

■ Use the details to write a story about an event in history. Make your characters act, talk, and dress like people who lived during that time.

Title:_____

1. Tell when and where the event happened and who was there.

The year was _____. _____

and _____ were at the _____

_____

in _____.

2. Tell what your characters did and said.

_____

_____

_____

_____

_____

_____

_____

_____

_____

_____

_____

3. Tell what finally happened.

_____

_____

_____

_____

© Hampton-Brown

Revising

📖 Use Handbook pages 100–102.

Revise this story. Be sure the details tell
about the past.

Revising Marks	
∧	Add.
⟋⟍	Move to here.
⟋⌐	Replace with this.
⟍	Take out.
⊙	Add a period.

The first Thanksgiving feast was about to begin at the

restaurant. Mother was cooking a wild bird called a turkey in the

oven and fixing some frozen corn-on-the-cob. We were getting out

the plastic bowls and plates.

"We wouldn't have all this food if the Wampanoag hadn't helped

us the winter. They taught us how to do things," said Mother.

Editing and
Proofreading

📖 Use Handbook page 106.

Proofread this story. Be sure
to use nouns and punctuation
in the dialogue correctly.

Proofreading Marks			
∧	Add.	◯	Check spelling.
⋏	Add a comma.	⟋	Make lowercase.
⊙	Add a period.	¶	Start a new paragraph.
≡	Capitalize.	⟍	Take out.

"What are you doing up there? asked Robert Smith. He was

watching several man throwing thing off a ship in Boston Harbor.

We're protesting the many unfair tax on tea" they said. Maybe

the British will listen to us if we dump these box of tea into the

harbor. "You are very brave to protest like this for our

independence" said Robert. "May I join you?"

© Hampton-Brown

Drafting

📖 Use Handbook page 97.

- Look at the notes you took during your interview.
- Write a report to share what you learned.

An Interview with _____

by _____

Why did you decide to volunteer?

Q: _____ ?

A: _____

_____

_____ .

Q: _____ ?

A: _____

_____

_____ .

Q: _____ ?

A: _____

_____

_____ .

Q: _____ ?

A: _____

_____

_____ .

© Hampton-Brown

Revising

📖 Use Handbook pages 100–102.

Revise this report from an interview.
Be sure the details are correct.

Revising Marks	
∧	Add.
⟳	Move to here.
⤺	Replace with this.
⤶	Take out.
⊙	Add a period.

Questions to Ask Derek Johnson

What do you do at the Midtown Food Bank?

Well, I pick up donated canned goods from grocery stores. Then I take the food to people who need it.

How many hours do you volunteer?

I'm usually busy about 4 hours every Saturday. Every minute is worth it, though. I love helping people.

An Interview

Q: **What do you do at the Food Bank?**

A: I buy canned goods from grocery stores.

Then I take the food to people who need it.

Q: **How many hours do you volunteer?**

A: He's usually busy about 2 hours every

Saturday. Every minute is worth it, though.

I love people. Especially the people I work for.

Editing and Proofreading

📖 Use Handbook page 106.

Proofread this part of a report from an interview. Fix the punctuation and verb tenses.

Proofreading Marks			
∧	Add.	⟲	Check spelling.
⋏	Add a comma.	/	Make lowercase.
⊙	Add a period.	¶	Start a new paragraph.
≡	Capitalize.	⤶	Take out.

Diane Hollis volunteered a few hours every week at the Humane

Society? I asked her, "Why do you volunteer" Diane said, I love

animals and it made me sad to see them so lonely. Animals always

liked getting lots of attention.

© Hampton-Brown

English
At Your Command!

Student
Progress
Test

Vocabulary

Mark the answer that means about the same thing as the underlined part. The sample has been done for you.

Sample

The lifeguard was <u>concerned</u> about the big waves.

- ⬭ amused
- ⬭ interested
- ⬭ surprised
- ⬛ worried

---

1 Did the missing cat <u>turn up</u> yet?
- ⬭ appear
- ⬭ look up
- ⬭ run away
- ⬭ turn over

2 She will <u>look over</u> the homework tomorrow.
- ⬭ copy
- ⬭ pick up
- ⬭ review
- ⬭ turn in

3 The boys <u>spilled the beans about the party</u>.
- ⬭ ate a meal at the party
- ⬭ cooked beans for the party
- ⬭ made a mess at the party
- ⬭ told people the party was happening

4 I always <u>hit the books</u> before a test.
- ⬭ eat
- ⬭ go to bed early
- ⬭ go to the library
- ⬭ study

5 Junji found some <u>inexpensive</u> toys at the yard sale.
- ⬭ broken
- ⬭ cheap
- ⬭ costly
- ⬭ special

6 I had to <u>disconnect</u> the wires.
- ⬭ attach
- ⬭ take apart
- ⬭ tie in a knot
- ⬭ throw away

7 The path went <u>upward</u>.
- ⬭ to the bottom
- ⬭ to the inside
- ⬭ to the middle
- ⬭ to the top

8 Some people <u>weep</u> at the movies.
- ⬭ cry
- ⬭ eat
- ⬭ laugh
- ⬭ sleep

9 The statue had been buried for <u>a century</u>.
- ⬭ one hundred years
- ⬭ one thousand years
- ⬭ ten years
- ⬭ twenty years

GO ON ➡

---

10 Recess ends at <u>quarter past</u> ten.
- ○ nine forty-five
- ○ nine thirty
- ○ ten fifteen
- ○ ten twenty-five

11 The sky looks lovely at <u>dusk</u>.
- ○ daybreak
- ○ midnight
- ○ noon
- ○ sunset

12 I go to the dentist <u>semiannually</u>.
- ○ every two years
- ○ monthly
- ○ two times in a year
- ○ yearly

13 We go hiking when the weather is <u>fair</u>.
- ○ clear and sunny
- ○ good for rides and games
- ○ the same for all

14 The <u>bat</u> cracked when she hit a home run.
- ○ long wooden stick
- ○ small flying animal
- ○ small round ball

15 My <u>ring</u> has a shiny green stone.
- ○ sound a bell makes
- ○ large circle
- ○ piece of jewelry

16 This torn bag is <u>useless</u>.
- ○ ugly
- ○ not good for anything
- ○ helpful

Mark the answer that best completes the sentence.

17 The sail on this boat is shaped like _____.
- ○ a diamond
- ○ a rectangle
- ○ a triangle
- ○ an oval

18 The _____ sock has stripes on it.
- ○ fifth
- ○ fifty
- ○ five
- ○ fourth

19 The mouse is _____ the pumpkins.
- ○ behind
- ○ below
- ○ between
- ○ inside

20 It's hard to _____ on a foggy night.
- ○ sea
- ○ see

21 Let's take the road _____ town.
- ○ threw
- ○ through

22 Our team won the _____ competition!
- ○ national
- ○ nation

© Hampton-Brown

Organizing Ideas

Read each item and mark your answer. The sample has been done for you.

Sample

Which of these would you use to make a word web?

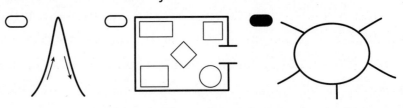

1 Look at this diagram. It is most useful for showing
   - ⬭ four steps in a process
   - ⬭ how details are related to a main idea
   - ⬭ the ways in which two things are alike

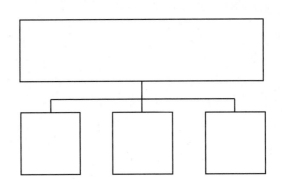

2 Which of these would <u>not</u> be used to show the sequence of events?

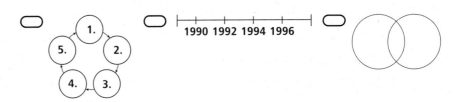

3 Which of these would you use to show how a bird and a turtle are alike and different?

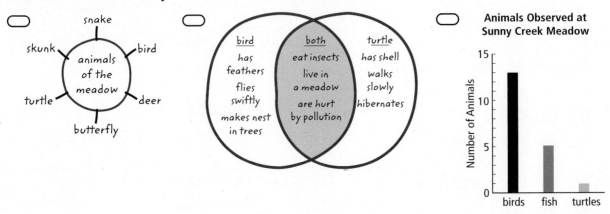

GO ON ➡

Read the paragraph. Then find the graphic organizer that best shows what the paragraph is about.

Alvar Nuñez Cabeza de Vaca was born in southern Spain in 1490. Like his grandfathers, Alvar became a soldier and was soon known for his bravery. In 1527, the King of Spain sent him to explore Florida, in North America. The trip was a disaster. Only four of the men survived, but Cabeza de Vaca did not give up. He led the other three men on a walk across the unfamiliar land. That journey lasted eight years and covered hundreds of miles!

4 ○ kept a journal — sailed to Brazil — Cabeza de Vaca — marched 1,000 miles across South America — loyal to King — died in Spain

○ Spanish — a leader — Cabeza de Vaca — brave soldier — didn't give up — strong

○ sailor — brave — Cabeza de Vaca — strong — bilingual — good rider

To make candles, first melt some wax in a tall tin can inside a pot of boiling water. While the wax melts, cut wicks to the length you want. Then, dip the wick into the melted wax and pull it out. Next, dip the wick into a can of cold water to cool it. Continue dipping into the hot wax and then into the cold water until the candle is as thick as you want it to be. Be sure to work with a grown-up, because hot wax is dangerous!

5 ○
| 1. Melt wax. | 2. Cut candle wicks. | 3. Dip wick in wax. | 4. Dip wick in cold water. | 5. Repeat Steps 3 and 4 until candle is as big as you want. |

○
| 1. Melt wax. | 2. Dip a wick in wax. | 3. Cut the wick. | 4. Dip wick in cold water. | 5. Repeat Steps 2 and 3. |

○
| 1. Melt wax. | 2. Cut candle wicks. | 3. Dip wick in cold water. | 4. Dip wick in wax. | 5. Continue dipping in water until candle is as big as you want. |

STOP

Writing

Choose a season of the year. Think about what it is like and what people do during that time of year. Write a description of that season. Also, tell what you think or feel about the season. Be sure to include colorful verbs and words that describe.

Winter

Fall

Spring

Summer

STOP

Think of a gift you have received, or imagine one you would like to get. Write a thank-you note to say "thank you" for the gift. Be sure to include the date, greeting, and closing in your letter.

Spelling

Mark the correct spelling of each word to complete the sentence. The sample has been done for you.

Sample

Omar is _____ in the park.
- ⬭ joging
- ⬭ joggin
- ⬬ jogging
- ⬭ joggng

1 This box is _____ than that box.
- ⬭ larjer
- ⬭ larger
- ⬭ largeer
- ⬭ largger

2 Saturday is the _____ day of the week.
- ⬭ busiest
- ⬭ buziest
- ⬭ busyest
- ⬭ busyiest

3 Benjamin Franklin _____ the wood stove.
- ⬭ inventted
- ⬭ inventeed
- ⬭ invented
- ⬭ inventid

4 I am _____ about my math test.
- ⬭ nervus
- ⬭ nerveous
- ⬭ nerveus
- ⬭ nervous

5 The cook is _____ an egg.
- ⬭ frying
- ⬭ fryeing
- ⬭ fryng
- ⬭ fryyng

6 Juanita _____ her room yesterday.
- ⬭ clend
- ⬭ cleaned
- ⬭ cleant
- ⬭ cleanned

7 We _____ about the movie.
- ⬭ disagree
- ⬭ disgree
- ⬭ disaggree
- ⬭ dissagree

8 That yellow rose is _____!
- ⬭ beautifull
- ⬭ beautyful
- ⬭ beautful
- ⬭ beautiful

9 The children are sleeping _____.
- ⬭ comfortablely
- ⬭ comfortably
- ⬭ comfortabley
- ⬭ comfortablly

10 I see many _____ sheep on the hill.
- ⬭ woolly
- ⬭ woolley
- ⬭ woolie
- ⬭ wooley

11 Please turn off the _____ in the living room.
- ⬭ lampes
- ⬭ lamps
- ⬭ lampps
- ⬭ lampses

GO ON ➡

12 These _____ are juicy and sweet.
- ⃝ peaches
- ⃝ peachis
- ⃝ peachs
- ⃝ peachez

13 There are a lot of _____ around the barn.
- ⃝ flyes
- ⃝ flies
- ⃝ flys
- ⃝ fliez

14 Can you swim _____ the pool?
- ⃝ across
- ⃝ akross
- ⃝ accross
- ⃝ ucross

15 Let's ride our bikes on the _____.
- ⃝ side walk
- ⃝ sidwalk
- ⃝ sidewak
- ⃝ sidewalk

16 Josh picks up paper clips with a _____.
- ⃝ magnut
- ⃝ magnit
- ⃝ magnet
- ⃝ maggnet

17 Did you read the _____ about birds?
- ⃝ artikle
- ⃝ article
- ⃝ artical
- ⃝ articul

18 Molly _____ ten books last summer.
- ⃝ reed
- ⃝ red
- ⃝ readed
- ⃝ read

19 Here is _____ raincoat, Alex.
- ⃝ yore
- ⃝ your
- ⃝ you're
- ⃝ yur

20 I have a dog. I have a fish, _____.
- ⃝ two
- ⃝ to
- ⃝ tew
- ⃝ too

21 The cat licks _____ paw.
- ⃝ it's
- ⃝ its
- ⃝ itts
- ⃝ its'

22 Tran and Anil lost _____ tickets to the show.
- ⃝ there
- ⃝ thair
- ⃝ their
- ⃝ they're

STOP

Language

Read each paragraph. Then read the question about each underlined part. Mark your answer. The sample has been done for you.

Sample

The armadillo are an interesting animal. The female always has four babies, and
        S
they are either all boys or all girls!

S Which of these is the best way to write Part S?
- ○ Armadillos is an interesting animal.
- ● The armadillo is an interesting animal.
- ○ Best as it is.

You may have heard of Lewis and Clark, and does you ever hear of Sacagawea?
                                        1
She. Was a young Shoshone mother who helped Lewis and Clark on their Expedition.
        2
Sacagawea helping to get horses from the Shoshone people. Without no horses,
        3   4
the Expedition could not cross the Rocky Mountains.

1 Which of these is the best way to write Part 1?
- ○ Lewis and Clark, but does you ever hear
- ○ Lewis and Clark, so did you ever hear
- ○ Lewis and Clark, but did you ever hear
- ○ Best as it is.

2 Which of these is the best way to write Part 2?
- ○ She was. A young Shoshone mother
- ○ She was a young Shoshone mother
- ○ She a young Shoshone mother
- ○ Best as it is.

3 Which of these is the best way to write Part 3?
- ○ Sacagawea helped to get horses
- ○ Sacagawea helps to get horses
- ○ Sacagawea been helping to get horses
- ○ Best as it is.

4 Which of these is the best way to write Part 4?
- ○ Not with any horses,
- ○ With any horses,
- ○ Without any horses,
- ○ Best as it is.

GO ON

The word *zero* means "nothing." You or I both know that. But do you know where the
<u>5</u> <u>6</u>
zero was first used? <u>The Mayans was probably the first people</u> to use the zero, around the
<u>7</u>
year 300. Several hundred years <u>later, the zero begin to be used</u> in India. Before I heard this
<u>8</u>
story, <u>I am thinking our ancient cultures</u> were very smart. Now I <u>have learned</u> that's true!
<u>9</u> <u>10</u>

5 Which of these is the best way to write Part 5?
- ⬭ The word *zero*.
- ⬭ The word *zero* means.
- ⬭ Means "nothing."
- ⬭ Best as it is.

6 Which of these is the best way to write Part 6?
- ⬭ You and I both know that.
- ⬭ You and me both know that.
- ⬭ I or you both know that.
- ⬭ Best as it is.

7 Which of these is the best way to write Part 7?
- ⬭ The Mayans is probably the first people
- ⬭ The Mayans were probably the first people
- ⬭ The Mayans will probably be the first people
- ⬭ Best as it is.

8 Which of these is the best way to write Part 8?
- ⬭ later, the zero began to be used
- ⬭ later, the zero begins to be used
- ⬭ later, the zero beginning to be used
- ⬭ Best as it is.

9 Which of these is the best way to write part 9?
- ⬭ was thought our ancient cultures
- ⬭ think our ancient cultures
- ⬭ had thought our ancient cultures
- ⬭ Best as it is.

10 Which is the best way to write part 10?
- ⬭ had learned
- ⬭ will learned
- ⬭ was learning
- ⬭ Best as it is.

GO ON ➡

Language

Mark the answer that is written correctly.

11 ◯ The buses wheels were large.
◯ The bus's wheels were large.
◯ The bus' wheels were large.

12 ◯ Our family take a trip last summer.
◯ Our family takes a trip last summer.
◯ Our family took a trip last summer.

13 ◯ This are my favorite books.
◯ This is my favorite books.
◯ These are my favorite books.

14 ◯ Our school starts in September.
◯ Our school starts in the September.
◯ Our school starts in the september.

15 ◯ Please pass your sister the salad. He wants it.
◯ Please pass your sister the salad. She wants it.
◯ Please pass your sister the salad. She wants them.

16 ◯ You and I play soccer. We are on the same team.
◯ You and I play soccer. We is on the same team.
◯ You and I play soccer. They are on the same team.

17 ◯ The dog wants to take a walk. Please get it's leash.
◯ The dog wants to take a walk. Please get its leash.
◯ The dog wants to take a walk. Please get their leash.

18 ◯ Nico is the fastest runner.
◯ Nico is the more faster runner.
◯ Nico is the most fastest runner.

19 ◯ At the party, there will be a lot of the dancing.
◯ At the party, there will be a lot of dancing.
◯ At the party, there will be a lot of dancings.

20 ◯ I will have some milk with my soup.
◯ I will have some milks with my soup.
◯ I will have some milks with my soups.

STOP

Mechanics

Read the paragraph. Then read the question about each underlined part. Mark your answer. The sample has been done for you.

Sample

Nuts grow in almost every area of the <u>World. Hawaii</u> is famous for macadamia nuts.
S

S Which shows the correct way to write Part S?

  ⬭ World Hawaii   ⬤ world. Hawaii   ⬭ world. hawaii   ⬭ Correct as it is.

The cherry blossom is <u>japans national flower.</u> <u>The people of japan</u> celebrate the return
1 2

of the <u>cherry blossom's each spring</u> with dances and songs. <u>Japanese americans also</u>
3 4

celebrate the arrival of <u>the beautiful delicate blossoms.</u> <u>In San francisco California,</u> the
5 6

celebration is held in April. <u>It includes karate dancing and crafts.</u>
7

1 Which shows the correct way to write Part 1?
  ⬭ Japans national flower.
  ⬭ Japan's national flower.
  ⬭ Correct as it is.

2 Which shows the correct way to write Part 2?
  ⬭ The People of japan
  ⬭ The people of Japan
  ⬭ Correct as it is.

3 Which shows the correct way to write Part 3?
  ⬭ cherry blossoms each spring
  ⬭ cherry blossoms' each spring
  ⬭ Correct as it is.

4 Which shows the correct way to write Part 4?
  ⬭ japanese Americans also
  ⬭ Japanese Americans also
  ⬭ Correct as it is.

5 Which shows the correct way to write Part 5?
  ⬭ the beautiful, delicate blossoms.
  ⬭ the beautiful delicate, blossoms.
  ⬭ Correct as it is.

6 Which shows the correct way to write Part 6?
  ⬭ In San Francisco California,
  ⬭ In San Francisco, California,
  ⬭ Correct as it is.

7 Which shows the correct way to write Part 7?
  ⬭ It includes karate, dancing, and crafts.
  ⬭ It includes, karate, dancing, and crafts.
  ⬭ Correct as it is.

GO ON ➡️

Read the letter. Then read the question about each underlined part. Mark your answer.

375 Timber Lake Lane
pine grove, Ca 95390
—————————
8
July 19, 2002

Dear Ms. Bauers,

I have some exciting news for you There is a piano at the cabin where we are
————————————————————
9

staying. and I have been practicing every day. Do you know why It's because the weather
———————————————————— ——————————————
10   11

has been terrible. By last Saturday I had learned my favorite song by heart. Please add
————————————————
12

Moonlight Sonata to the program for the fall concert. I'll be ready to play it!
————————————   ———————————————————
13   14

Your student:
————————
15
Sylvia Lessem

8 Which shows the correct way to write Part 8?
- ⬭ Pine grove, Ca 95390
- ⬭ Pine Grove, CA 95390
- ⬭ Correct as it is.

9 Which shows the correct way to write Part 9?
- ⬭ news for you! There is a piano
- ⬭ news for you? There is a piano
- ⬭ Correct as it is.

10 Which shows the correct way to write Part 10?
- ⬭ staying. And I have been practicing
- ⬭ staying, and I have been practicing
- ⬭ Correct as it is.

11 Which shows the correct way to write Part 11?
- ⬭ Do you know why.
- ⬭ Do you know why?
- ⬭ Correct as it is.

12 Which shows the correct way to write Part 12?
- ⬭ By last saturday, i had
- ⬭ By last Saturday, I had
- ⬭ Correct as it is.

13 Which shows the correct way to write Part 13?
- ⬭ "Moonlight Sonata"
- ⬭ Moonlight "Sonata"
- ⬭ Correct as it is.

14 Which shows the correct way to write Part 14?
- ⬭ I'l be ready to play it!
- ⬭ Il'l be ready to play it!
- ⬭ Correct as it is.

15 Which shows the correct way to write Part 15?
- ⬭ Your student.
- ⬭ Your student,
- ⬭ Correct as it is.

Research Skills

Use this part of a dictionary page to answer each question. Mark your answer.

fortification ⟩ **foundation**

fortification 1. The act of strengthening something: *a wall built as part of the fortification of the town.* 2. Something that strengthens, such as a wall or embankment. **for·ti·fi·ca·tion** (fôr′tə fi kā′shən) *noun, plural* **fortifications.**

fortify 1. To make stronger or more secure: *They fortified the town by building high walls around it* 2. To add strengthening ingredients to: enrich: *This breakfast cereal is fortified with vitamins and iron.* **for·ti·fy** (fôr′tə fi) *verb,* **fortified, fortifying.**

fortress A strong place that can be defended against attack; fort. **for·tress** (fôr′tris) *noun, plural* **fortresses.**

fortunate Having or resulting from good luck; lucky: *One fortunate person has won the contest twice.* **for·tu·nate** (fôr′chə nit) *adjective*

forwards Another spelling for the adverb forward. **for·wards** (fôr′wərdz) *adverb.*

fossil The hardened remains or traces of an animal or plant that lived long ago: *The fossils we found were imprints of ancient seashells in rock.* **fos·sil** (fos′əl) *noun, plural* **fossils.**

fossil fuel A fuel formed from the remains of prehistoric plants and animals. Coal and petroleum are fossil fuels.

foster To help the growth or development of: *My parents fostered my interest in music. Verb.* ○ Giving or receiving care in a family without being related by birth or adoption: *The state has a special department that tries to find foster parents for homeless children. Adjective.* **fos·ter** (fos′tər) *verb,* **fostered, fostering;** *adjective.*

fought Past t...

1 What will be the last entry on this page?
- ⬭ forwards
- ⬭ fought
- ⬭ foundation

2 Which of these gives correct information about the word *fortification*?
- ⬭ It is an entry word.
- ⬭ It is a guide word.
- ⬭ It is a guide word and an entry word.

3 What part of speech is the word *forwards*?
- ⬭ adjective
- ⬭ adverb
- ⬭ verb

4 If the word *forty* were added to this page, which word would come right before it?
- ⬭ fortunate
- ⬭ forwards
- ⬭ fought

5 Which of these entries does <u>not</u> include a sample sentence?
- ⬭ fortify
- ⬭ fortunate
- ⬭ fossil fuel

6 According to the definitions on the dictionary page, which of these is true?
- ⬭ A fortress is impossible to defend.
- ⬭ A fortunate person has good luck.
- ⬭ A fossil is a live plant.

GO ON ➡

Research Skills

Read this encyclopedia article.

422 Fossil

© Catherine Ursillo, Photo Researchers

Fossils, such as these dinosaur skeletons, help museum visitors visualize ancient species. Scientists study fossils to learn about the development and ways of life of prehistoric organisms.

Fossil

Fossil is the mark or remains of a plant or animal that lived thousands or millions of years ago. Some fossils are leaves, shells, or skeletons that were preserved after a plant or animal died. Others are tracks or trails left by moving animals.

Most fossils are found in *sedimentary rocks*. These fossils formed from plant or animal remains that were quickly buried in *sediments*—the mud or sand that collects at the bottom of rivers, lakes, swamps, and oceans. After thousands of years, the weight of upper layers of sediment pressing down on the lower layers turned them into rock (see **Sedimentary rock**). A few fossils are whole plants or animals that have been preserved in ice, tar, or hardened sap.

The oldest fossils are microscopic traces of bacteria that scientists believe lived about $3\frac{1}{2}$ billion years ago. The oldest animal fossils are remains of *invertebrates* (animals without a backbone) estimated to be about 700 million years old. The oldest fossils of *vertebrates* (animals with a backbone) are fossil fish about 500 million years old.

Steven M. Stanley, the contributor of this article, is Professor of Earth and Planetary Sciences at The Johns Hopkins University. He has written several books on paleontology.

Fossils are more common and easier to find than many people realize. For example, fossils are plentiful in nearly every state in the United States. Even so, scientists believe that only a small portion of the countless plants and animals that have lived on earth have been preserved as fossils. Many species are thought to have lived and died without leaving any trace whatsoever in the fossil record.

Although the fossil record is incomplete, many important groups of animals and plants have left fossil remains. These fossils help scientists discover what forms of life existed at various periods in the past and how these prehistoric species lived. Fossils also indicate how life on earth has gradually changed over time. This article explains how fossils provide information on ancient life. For a description of animals of the past, see **Prehistoric animal**; for a description of early human beings, see **Prehistoric people**.

How fossils reveal the past

In the distant past, when most fossils formed, the world was different from today. Plants and animals that have long since vanished inhabited the waters and land. A region now covered with high mountains may have been the floor of an ancient sea. Where a lush tropical forest thrived millions of years ago, there may now be a cool, dry plain. Even the continents have drifted far from the positions they occupied hundreds of millions

GO ON ➡️

© Hampton-Brown

Use the encyclopedia article to answer these questions. Mark your answer. The sample has been done for you.

Sample

Which of these articles would appear in the same volume as "Fossil"?

- ⬭ Desert
- ⬛ Fish
- ⬭ Reptiles

---

7 Which of these is the entry word?

- ⬭ Dinosaur
- ⬭ Fossil
- ⬭ How fossils reveal the past

8 Which of these is <u>not</u> a fossil?

- ⬭ leaves
- ⬭ sediment
- ⬭ shells
- ⬭ skeletons

9 Which article should you read to find information on early humans?

- ⬭ Prehistoric animals
- ⬭ Prehistoric people
- ⬭ Sedimentary rock

10 Using the information in the text, which of these is true?

- ⬭ The oldest fossils found are vertebrates.
- ⬭ The oldest fossils found are microscopic bacteria.
- ⬭ The oldest fossils found are invertebrates.

Read each of these items about doing research. Mark your answer.

11 What is the first step in the research process?

- ⬭ locating resources
- ⬭ deciding what to look up
- ⬭ choosing a topic
- ⬭ organizing information

12 Which of these words comes just before **orchestra** in alphabetical order?

- ⬭ order
- ⬭ orcus
- ⬭ orchard
- ⬭ orchid

13 When you are skimming an article, it is <u>not</u> important to read the

- ⬭ title
- ⬭ whole thing
- ⬭ headings
- ⬭ ending paragraph

14 When you take notes, it is <u>not</u> important to

- ⬭ put quotation marks around the words you copy
- ⬭ put your research question at the top of your card
- ⬭ write down every word
- ⬭ write down the source of the information

15 Which of these would you use to find the pages in a book that contain information about your topic?

- ⬭ copyright page
- ⬭ index
- ⬭ glossary
- ⬭ title page

Name _____ Date _____

Self-Assessment Form

**Look at the writing in your portfolio. Use this form
to help you think about how you're doing as a writer.**

What kinds of writing did you do?

_____

_____

Which piece of writing is your favorite? Why do you like it?

_____

_____

How is your first piece of writing different from your last?

_____

_____

What have you learned about your writing? What do you like to write about?
What kinds of sentences or words do you like to use?

_____

_____

What is hard for you? Mark the things you need to work on.

☐ Choosing the right words   ☐ Organizing ideas before I write

☐ Making my writing clear, organized,   ☐ Finding information and doing
   and interesting   research

☐ Using the English language correctly, especially _____ .

☐ Other. Explain: _____

_____

What will you do the next time to help you do your best writing?

_____

_____